SPAIN

ABDO
Publishing Company

SPAIN

by Marcia Amidon Lusted

Content Consultant
Luis Alvarez-Castro
Associate Professor of Spanish
University of Florida

CREDITS

Published by ABDO Publishing Company, PO Box 398166, Minneapolis, MN 55439.
Copyright © 2013 by Abdo Consulting Group, Inc. International copyrights reserved
in all countries. No part of this book may be reproduced in any form without written
permission from the publisher. The Essential Library™ is a trademark and logo of ABDO
Publishing Company.

Printed in the United States of America,
North Mankato, Minnesota
112012
012013

 THIS BOOK CONTAINS AT LEAST 10% RECYCLED MATERIALS.

Editor: Arnold Ringstad
Series Designer: Emily Love

About the Author: Marcia Amidon Lusted is the author of more than 70 books for
young readers, as well as more than 300 magazine articles. She has visited Spain, watched
a bullfight, and especially enjoyed exploring the Alhambra Palace and eating wonderful
Spanish food.

Cataloging-in-Publication Data

Lusted, Marcia Amidon.
 Spain / Marcia Amidon Lusted.
   p. cm. -- (Countries of the world)
Includes bibliographical references and index.
ISBN 978-1-61783-637-4
1. Spain--Juvenile literature.   I. Title.
946--dc22

2012946080

Cover: The Sagrada Família in Barcelona

TABLE OF CONTENTS

CHAPTER 1	A Visit to Spain	6
	Map: Political Boundaries of Spain	13
	Snapshot	15
CHAPTER 2	Geography: A Diverse Peninsula	16
	Map: Geography of Spain	19
	Map: Climate of Spain	27
CHAPTER 3	Animals and Nature: Species in Danger	28
CHAPTER 4	History: From Empires to a Republic	40
CHAPTER 5	People: United Diversity	62
	Map: Population Density of Spain	70
CHAPTER 6	Culture: Beyond Bullfights	74
CHAPTER 7	Politics: A Modern Monarchy	92
CHAPTER 8	Economics: Money Troubles	104
	Map: Resources of Spain	107
CHAPTER 9	Spain Today	116
TIMELINE		128
FACTS AT YOUR FINGERTIPS		130
GLOSSARY		134
ADDITIONAL RESOURCES		136
SOURCE NOTES		138
INDEX		142
PHOTO CREDITS		144

CHAPTER 1
A VISIT TO SPAIN

The air is warm, and even though it is late at night, the streets are alive with people. Music spills out from nightclubs, couples wander beneath glittering lights, and diners are just starting their evening meal. Art galleries, restaurants, and live music surround you. Through windows, you see people dancing in flamenco clubs and discos. You have arrived in Madrid, Spain's capital since 1561. You are close to the geographic center of Europe's Iberian Peninsula.

You stroll past the Prado Museum, one of the greatest art museums in the world. You look forward to seeing its collection of paintings by Francisco de Goya later in your trip. After walking for a few more minutes, you come across the Plaza Mayor in Madrid's historic old city. The plaza has been the central square of the city for hundreds of years. Stopping for a rest at one of the picturesque cafés, you sip espresso and eat a long thin doughnut called a churro, watching cars and people pass by. Nearby is the Royal Palace, built in the eighteenth century. It has an

The bustling metropolis of Madrid is Spain's largest city.

amazing 2,800 rooms and is surrounded by beautiful gardens.[1] Beside the palace is the Plaza de Oriente and the Teatro Real, or Royal Theater. Also nearby is the Puerta del Sol, or Gate of the Sun. Once simply one of the gates in the walls surrounding fifteenth-century Madrid, this square is now one of the most popular destinations in the city for locals and tourists alike.

A COUNTRY OF CONTRASTS

Though Madrid feels very European, traveling south to Granada reveals another of Spain's facets. Between the eighth and fifteenth centuries, the Muslims who conquered Spain constructed beautiful buildings in the Moorish style of architecture. The Alhambra Palace and the Generalife gardens in Granada feature ornate carved stonework that almost looks like lace. You walk through courtyards and alongside pools, where delicate fountains spray mist into the hot, dry air.

ALHAMBRA PALACE

Historians believe that Alhambra, Arabic for "the red," may have gotten its name from the red color of the surrounding hills. Others theorize the name comes from the fact that the palace was built by torchlight, which gave the walls a reddish color at night.

The Alhambra palace is representative of the Moorish architecture that dots Spain's countryside and cities.

Brightly colored mosaics adorn walls and floors, and nearby stands an old stone watchtower, once part of a fortress. You feel very far away from the quick pace of Madrid.

You explore Granada's old Muslim quarter, Albayzín. Its narrow cobblestone streets wind up a hill that faces the Moorish Alhambra Palace, across the Darro Valley. Donkeys trudge patiently up the streets, carrying loads on their backs. Albayzín is virtually an open-air museum of life in Granada during the period of Muslim rule. At the top of the hill is the Plaza del Salvador, once the location of the area's largest mosque. Today a sixteenth-century church stands in its place. Only the mosque's arched patio remains.

Granada's visible past reflects the growing Islamic population coming to the city from North Africa today. A new mosque has been built, and businesses such as kebab restaurants and tea shops are slowly filtering back into Albayzín.

Continuing your journey past Granada, heading southwest along the coast, you finally come to stand at the shore of the Strait of Gibraltar, a thin waterway threading between Spain and Morocco. From here you can see all the way to Africa and the city of Tangier, a reminder of Spain's North African influences.

Valencia is among the largest Mediterranean port cities.

WORK AND FUN

You then travel back northeast to explore Spain's Valencia region. With its coastal strip on the Mediterranean Sea, Valencia is where vacationers come to enjoy beachside resorts. Despite its dry climate, it is also an important agricultural region. The rich soil makes it easy to grow corn, wheat, rice, and fruit. However, due to water shortages, a Tribunal de las Aguas, or Water Court, regulates the rights of landowners to water. The court has been making decisions each Thursday at noon for hundreds of years.

Catalonia, Valencia's neighbor to the north, is an important trade and industrial center, and its biggest city, Barcelona, is the most important manufacturing city in Spain. In Catalonia, one can enjoy Mediterranean beaches, ski at the Baqueira-Beret resort, or climb Pica d'Estats, the region's highest peak. Here, you can see both Spain and France.

THE ROCK OF GIBRALTAR

One of Spain's most famous landmarks is not owned by the country at all. The Rock of Gibraltar is a huge limestone rock formation that lies off the southern tip of Spain. It is almost 1,400 feet (425 m) high and overlooks the Strait of Gibraltar.[2] The Rock of Gibraltar sits on the territory of Gibraltar, a 2.5-square mile (6.5 sq km) area of land owned by the United Kingdom since 1713.[3] Much of the territory is a nature reserve.

In ancient times, the rock was one of the two Pillars of Hercules. Historians are uncertain of the location of the other pillar. According to mythology, they marked the end of the known world. Beyond them, sailors would supposedly fall off the edge of the world.

A HISTORY OF SEPARATION

The Pyrenees mountain range stands between Spain and France. Before the age of modern travel, it helped isolate Spain from the rest of the European mainland. This history of separation,

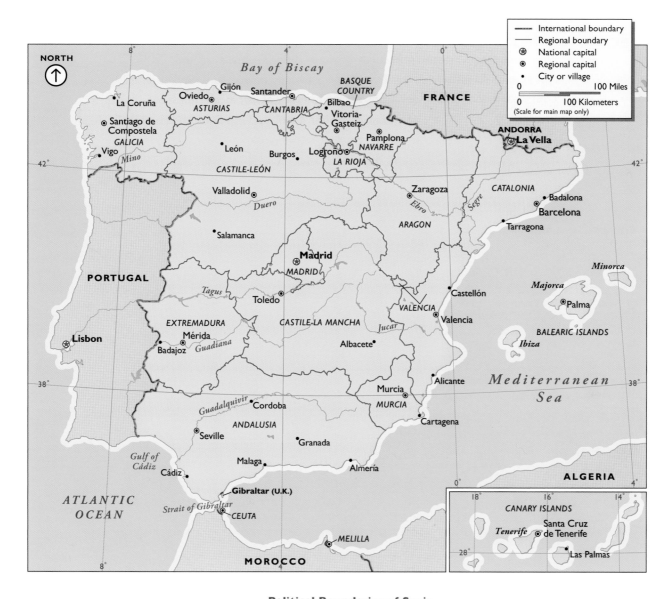

NORTH ↑

Bay of Biscay

BASQUE COUNTRY

FRANCE

La Coruña
Oviedo
Gijón
Santander
Bilbao
Vitoria-Gasteiz
ASTURIAS
CANTABRIA
Santiago de Compostela
GALICIA
Vigo
Miño
León
Burgos
Logroño
LA RIOJA
Pamplona
NAVARRE
ANDORRA
La Vella
CASTILE-LEÓN
Valladolid
Duero
Zaragoza
Ebro
Segre
ARAGON
CATALONIA
Badalona
Barcelona
Tarragona
Salamanca
PORTUGAL
Madrid
MADRID
Tagus
Toledo
EXTREMADURA
Mérida
Badajoz
Guadiana
CASTILE-LA MANCHA
Jucar
VALENCIA
Castellón
Valencia
Albacete
Minorca
Majorca
Palma
BALEARIC ISLANDS
Ibiza
Lisbon
Alicante
Mediterranean Sea
Guadalquivir
Cordoba
Murcia
MURCIA
Cartagena
ANDALUSIA
Seville
Granada
Gulf of Cádiz
Malaga
Almería
ALGERIA
Cádiz
Gibraltar (U.K.)
Strait of Gibraltar
CEUTA
ATLANTIC OCEAN
MELILLA
MOROCCO

CANARY ISLANDS
Tenerife
Santa Cruz de Tenerife
Las Palmas

Legend:
- - - - International boundary
——— Regional boundary
⊛ National capital
◉ Regional capital
• City or village

0 — 100 Miles
0 — 100 Kilometers
(Scale for main map only)

Political Boundaries of Spain

along with the influences of many different invaders and immigrants, has given Spain its many facets. And while the country is a vibrant nation in step with modern European life, many traces of earlier times and customs still remain. It is the visible contrast between the twenty-first century and the past that makes Spain a unique and fascinating place to explore.

Spain has more cell phones than people.

SNAPSHOT

Official name: Kingdom of Spain (Reino de España in Spanish)

Capital city: Madrid

Form of government: parliamentary monarchy

Title of leaders: prime minister (head of government); king (head of state)

Currency: euro

Population (July 2012 est.): 47,042,984
World rank: 27

Size: 195,124 square miles (505,370 sq km)
World rank: 52

Language: Spanish; Aranese, Basque, Catalan, and Galician are recognized regional languages

Official religion: none

Per capita GDP (2011, US dollars): $31,000
World rank: 43

CHAPTER 2

GEOGRAPHY: A DIVERSE PENINSULA

Spain covers most of the Iberian Peninsula. The country's area totals 195,124 square miles (505,370 sq km).[1] Jutting out into the North Atlantic Ocean, it helps form the Mediterranean Sea and the Bay of Biscay. The country of Portugal, stretching along Spain's western border, fills most of the remainder of the Iberian Peninsula. Spain is connected to Europe only at its northeast border with France, along the Pyrenees Mountains. Also bordering Spain are Andorra, which sits on the French border, and the tiny British territory of Gibraltar.

Spain's territory also includes several island groups. Among the largest are the Balearic Islands in the Mediterranean Sea, an archipelago that includes the islands of

The Strait of Gibraltar is 8 miles (12.9 km) wide at its narrowest point.

Spain's North Atlantic coast makes up the southern edge of the Bay of Biscay.

17

THE END OF THE EARTH

The Romans who occupied Spain referred to the Galicia region as *finis terrae*, or "the end of the earth," because it was the northwestern end of the landmass containing Europe, Africa, and Asia—the end of the known world at the time. The region, and particularly the port city of Finisterre, also earned the reputation as "the port of death" because so many ships left the port to sail west into unknown waters and never returned. Finisterre continues to be a working fishing port even today.

Majorca, Minorca, and Ibiza. Spain also owns the Canary Islands, located hundreds of miles southwest of the country, off the African coast. Three small islands off the coast of Morocco, collectively called the *plazas de soberanía*, or "places of sovereignty," are also Spanish. Spain's area also includes two cities in North Africa, Ceuta and Melilla. In all, Spain's land area is roughly twice that of the state of Oregon.[2]

REGIONS OF SPAIN

Spain is divided into 17 regions, called *comunidades autónomas*, or autonomous communities. Most lie on the Iberian Peninsula, including the Basque Country, Catalonia, Galicia, Andalusia, Asturias, Aragon, Cantabria, Castile-León, Castile-La Mancha, Extremadura, Madrid, Murcia, Navarre, La Rioja, and Valencia. The Balearic Islands and the Canary Islands are in the Mediterranean Sea and Atlantic Ocean, respectively. Besides its

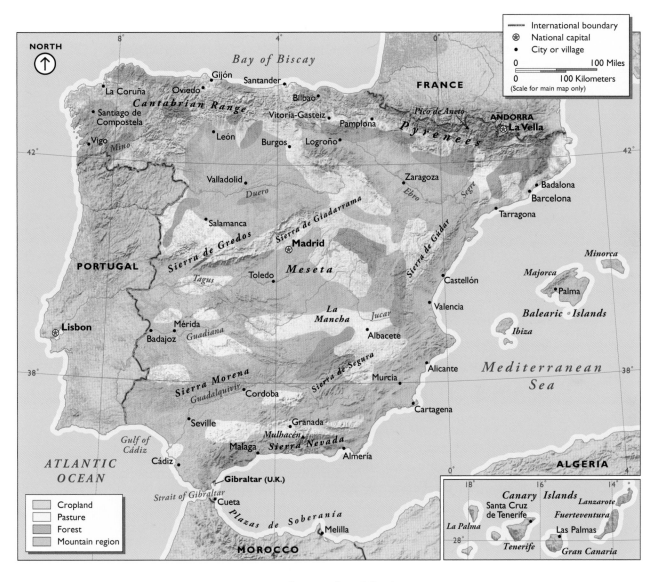

Geography of Spain

Map legend:
- International boundary
- National capital
- City or village

0 — 100 Miles
0 — 100 Kilometers
(Scale for main map only)

- Cropland
- Pasture
- Forest
- Mountain region

NORTH

Bay of Biscay

La Coruña
Oviedo
Gijón
Santander
Bílbao
Vitoria-Gasteiz
Pamplona
Santiago de Compostela
Cantabrian Range
León
Burgos
Logroño
Vigo
Mino

FRANCE
Pico de Aneto
ANDORRA
La Vella
Pyrenees

Zaragoza
Ebro
Segre
Badalona
Barcelona
Tarragona

Valladolid
Duero

Salamanca
Sierra de Gredos
Sierra de Giadarrama
Madrid
Meseta
Sierra de Gúdar

PORTUGAL
Tagus
Toledo

Castellón
Valencia
Minorca
Majorca
Palma
Balearic Islands
Ibiza

Lisbon
Mérida
Badajoz
Guadiana
La Mancha
Jucar
Albacete

Sierra Morena
Guadalquivir
Cordoba
Sierra de Segura
Murcia
Alicante

Mediterranean Sea

Seville
Granada
Mulhacén
Sierra Nevada
Malaga
Almería
Cádiz
Gulf of Cádiz

ATLANTIC OCEAN

ALGERIA

Gibraltar (U.K.)
Strait of Gibraltar
Cueta
Plazas de Soberania
Melilla

MOROCCO

Canary Islands
Santa Cruz de Tenerife
Lanzarote
Fuerteventura
La Palma
Las Palmas
Tenerife
Gran Canaria

17 regions, Spain also counts two autonomous cities, Ceuta and Melilla in North Africa, as part of its territory.

The drafters of Spain's 1978 Constitution divided Spain into these regions. The central government of Spain gave the regions five years of transition before they became completely autonomous. Each region is in control of its own institutions, public works, housing, cultural affairs, regional language, and health and social welfare, but there are lingering disputes with the central government of Spain regarding how much power each region retains. Some regions, such as the Basque Country and Catalonia, have more or different powers than other regions. These two regions are more industrial than the rest of the country. Many people within them see themselves as citizens of their regions first and foremost, rather than as Spanish citizens. The central Spanish government handles international relations, military affairs, and other aspects of governance beyond the scope of local regions.

SPAIN'S CITIES

Spain's two largest cities, Barcelona and Madrid, have historically performed roles that were neatly divided. Madrid, located near the geographic center of the country, has been the traditional center of government and administration. Barcelona, on the northeast coast, has been a center of commerce for thousands of years. Today, both cities

Barcelona is one of the largest cities on the Mediterranean coast.

The Ebro River passes through many Spanish cities and towns.

compete for a place in the international market. An intense soccer rivalry also exists between them. Madrid is the larger city, with more than 5.7 million people. Barcelona follows with just more than 5 million people.[3]

Other major Spanish cities include Valencia on the eastern coast, Granada in the south near the Sierra Nevada range, Seville in the southeast part of the country, and Cádiz on the southern coast, close to Africa. Valladolid and Zaragoza are major cities in the northwest and northeast, respectively.

PLATEAUS AND MOUNTAINS

Many diverse landscapes exist within Spain's borders. Most of the Iberian Peninsula is comprised of a high, flat plateau called the Meseta. It is divided into northern and southern areas. The large flat areas are divided by mountain ranges known as sierras, or "saws." The name comes from the way they cut up the plateaus. Spain's mountain ranges include the Cantabrian in the northwest, the Pyrenees in the northeast, the Sierra de Gredos and Sierra de Guadarrama cutting through the center of the Meseta, and the Sierra Morena and Sierra Nevada to the south. The Iberian Mountains cross the peninsula from north to south.

THE EBRO RIVER

The Ebro River ranks as the largest river in Spain by discharge volume, a measure of the amount of water flowing through it. It is also the longest river located entirely within Spain. It runs for 565 miles (910 km) from the Cantabrian Mountains in northern Spain to its delta in the Mediterranean Sea.[4] The Ebro has more than 200 tributaries and drains one-sixth of the country.[5] Some of these tributaries have been used to produce hydroelectric power, while others have been diverted for irrigation purposes.

The volcanoes of the Canary Islands feature
some of Spain's highest elevations.

Volcanoes formed the Canary Islands, and volcanic activity has been observed there as recently as 1971 on the islands of Tenerife and La Palma. The Balearic Islands feature small mountainous areas, several caves, and numerous bays.

AVERAGE TEMPERATURE AND PRECIPITATION

Region (City)	Average January Temperature Minimum/Maximum	Average July Temperature Minimum/Maximum	Average Precipitation January/July
Central (Madrid)	32/51°F (0/10°C)	61/90°F (16/32°C)	1.8/0.4 inches (4.6/1 cm)
Andalusia (Granada)	36/53°F (2/11°C)	64/90°F (17/32°C)	1.3/0.2 inches (3.3/0.5 cm)
Balearic Islands (Ibiza)	47/59°F (8/15°C)	70/84°F (21/29°C)	1.5/0.1 inches (3.8/0.3 cm)[7]
Northern (Santander)	46/54°F (7/12°C)	62/71°F (16/21°C)	4.1/1.8 inches (10.4/4.6 cm)[8]

Even though Spain's rivers, which include the Tagus, the Ebro, and the Duero, are among the longest in Europe, most of the country is very dry. Only 27 percent of Spain's land is used for agriculture, and large areas have to be irrigated in order to have enough water for crops.[6] Much of Spain suffers from frequent droughts, and much of the topsoil is blown away each year, making agriculture even more difficult.

CLIMATE

Spain's capital city, Madrid, sits in the northern end of the southern Meseta. The Meseta tends to have hot summers and cold winters. In summer, there are clear blue skies and blazing sunshine, with occasional thunderstorms. In contrast, the coastal areas of Spain tend to have more moderate weather, with cooler and cloudier summers, more rainfall, and milder winters. The Meseta also tends to be dry and arid, though regions to the north of it receive high rainfall.

The hottest temperature ever recorded in Spain was approximately 118°F (48°C).

Spain's Balearic Islands, sitting in the Mediterranean Sea, naturally have a temperate climate. Winters are mild, and temperatures never drop below freezing. Summers are hot, and sunshine is plentiful. The Canary Islands showcase a range of climatic conditions, depending on the prevailing winds, elevation, and distance to the ocean. Some areas are deserts, while others are covered with heavy vegetation—sometimes all on the same island.

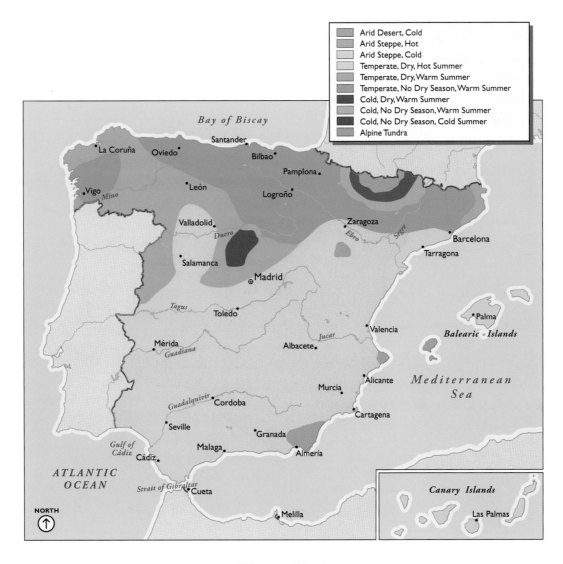

Legend:
- Arid Desert, Cold
- Arid Steppe, Hot
- Arid Steppe, Cold
- Temperate, Dry, Hot Summer
- Temperate, Dry, Warm Summer
- Temperate, No Dry Season, Warm Summer
- Cold, Dry, Warm Summer
- Cold, No Dry Season, Warm Summer
- Cold, No Dry Season, Cold Summer
- Alpine Tundra

Map labels:

Bay of Biscay

La Coruña, Santander, Oviedo, Bilbao, Pamplona, Vigo, *Mino*, León, Logroño, Zaragoza, *Ebro*, *Segre*, Barcelona, Valladolid, *Duero*, Tarragona, Salamanca, Madrid, *Tagus*, Toledo, *Jucar*, Valencia, Mérida, *Guadiana*, Albacete, *Balearic Islands*, Palma, Murcia, Alicante, *Mediterranean Sea*, *Guadalquivir*, Cordoba, Cartagena, Seville, Granada, *Gulf of Cádiz*, Malaga, Almería, Cádiz, ATLANTIC OCEAN, *Strait of Gibraltar*, Cueta, Melilla

NORTH

Canary Islands, Las Palmas

Climate of Spain

CHAPTER 3

ANIMALS AND NATURE: SPECIES IN DANGER

Culturally, the animal most closely associated with Spain is the bull. The Spanish traditions of bullfighting and of the running of the bulls are known across the world. However, bulls are found in nearly every country on Earth. There is another animal closely identified with Spain that is unique to the Iberian Peninsula: the Spanish imperial eagle. This large eagle is found in the forests and marshes of central and southwestern Spain. Individuals have wingspans ranging from 5.9 to 6.9 feet (1.8 to 2.1 m), and they can weigh as much as 7.7 pounds (3.5 kg). The Spanish imperial eagle is described as a vulnerable species by the International Union for Conservation of Nature. The greatest threats against these birds are power line electrocution and poisoning by humans.

Bulls hold an iconic place in Spanish culture, though they are just one of a great variety of species found in Spain.

A WIDE VARIETY

Because of the many different climates and terrains, animals found in Spain vary widely from one area to another. Additionally, the mountainous barrier between Spain and the rest of Europe has resulted in the existence of indigenous species that are found only in Spain. The country's proximity to Africa has also allowed species to migrate to Spain across the Strait of Gibraltar.

Spain is home to 90 species of mammals, but only 20 of these species are endemic to the country.[1] Brown bears and European wolves live in the forested northern regions, along with elk, roe deer, ibex, and wild boar. One elusive and endangered forest animal is the Iberian lynx. It survives on a variety of local rodents, including mice, hare, squirrels, and rabbits. Other mammals found in Spain include ermine, bats, and shrews.

In Gibraltar, the Barbary macaque can be found. The species, which

THE BARBARY MACAQUE

The Barbary macaque was most likely introduced to Gibraltar by the Romans or the Moors in ancient times and is not native to the area. Legend has it that as long as Barbary macaques live in Gibraltar, the British will control the territory.

A Barbary macaque looks out over Gibraltar.

ENDANGERED SPECIES IN SPAIN

According to the International Union for Conservation of Nature (IUCN), Spain is home to the following numbers of species that are categorized by the organization as Critically Endangered, Endangered, or Vulnerable:

Mammals	16
Birds	9
Reptiles	19
Amphibians	6
Fishes	71
Mollusks	140
Other Invertebrates	39
Plants	214
Total	514[2]

originated in Africa, is a small tailless monkey with tan fur and a bald pink face. It lives on the ground rather than in trees. They grow to approximately 24 inches (61 cm) in length and weigh up to 35 pounds (16 kg). Most Barbary macaques live in the mountains of Algeria and Morocco, but a small population lives at Gibraltar.

Spain's coastal areas and ocean waters are home to many different species, including whales, porpoises, and dolphins. Otters tend to be found along rivers or in estuaries, where rivers meet the sea. Several types of seals live along the coast and can be seen basking on warm rocks along the shore. In the water, jellyfish, sea urchins, sharks, and stingrays can pose a danger to humans. Fish species include red mullet, tuna, mackerel, pilchard, anchovies, and swordfish.

Spain is also known as a great place for bird watching. Besides the Spanish imperial eagle, birds found only in Spain include the blue chaffinch, the Fuerteventura stonechat, the Canary Islands chiffchaff, and the Balearic shearwater. The Canarian oystercatcher, once endemic to the Canary Islands, is now extinct. Spain is also home to birds such as vultures, eagles, kites, buzzards, storks, and flamingos.

THREATENED ANIMALS

Spain has many threatened species. The list includes vulnerable species such as the Canary big-eared bat, the harbor porpoise, and the Barbary sheep. Endangered species include the European mink and the northern right whale. The lava mouse, once found in the Canary Islands, is now extinct. Most critically endangered is the Mediterranean monk seal, which used to be plentiful in Spain and other parts of the Mediterranean but is now only found in small, scattered colonies. These seals can grow to more than 650 pounds (295 kg) and eight feet (2.4 m) in length and are covered in short, dark hairs. Hunting has reduced the seal's population drastically. The Mediterranean monk seal has also been threatened by entanglement in fishing gear, the loss of its habitat, and toxic algae on the ocean's surface.

The Iberian lynx is the most threatened species of wildcat in the world. These lynxes have gray or yellow-brown coats and dark, leopard-like spots. Their fur is shorter than that of other lynx species. Scientists estimate there are less than 300 individuals left in the wild.[3] Iberian lynx live in forests and pastures and hunt at night. Their decreasing numbers are linked to the decrease in rabbit populations, their primary food source, due to disease. The lynx has also suffered from illegal hunting, from being hit by cars, and from being inadvertently poisoned by hunters.

THE ENDANGERED IBERIAN LYNX

Hollywood actor Antonio Banderas, born in Andalusia, Spain, is just one of many people who have signed the Andalusian Pact for the Lynx. The aim of the pact is to persuade regional authorities to take the necessary actions to save the world's most endangered cat. Banderas has also coproduced an animated movie called *The Missing Lynx* to help publicize the animal's plight.

PLANT LIFE IN SPAIN

Just as Spain's animal population reflects its geographic diversity, so do its trees, plants, and flowers. Only a small amount of Spain's area is classified as woodland. In northern Spain, there are forests of oak and beech trees along with areas of open, uncultivated grassland. Mountains in the northern part of the Meseta have Portuguese oak trees, but mountains in the central Pyrenees and the Central Sierras are

The Iberian lynx is one of the rarest mammals in the world.

covered by several varieties of pine trees.

Outside of the mountains, much of the rest of the country has what is known as Mediterranean vegetation, consisting of broadleaf evergreens, bushes, and small trees such as the evergreen oak. Small plants resistant to drought are also found here, since the climate tends to be hot and dry. In the southeast, esparto grass grows. This hardy, gray-green, needlelike grass can survive in dry, sandy conditions. Esparto stems get tougher as they age, and have been used for making rope, paper, baskets, and sandals. Spain also has many species of flowers and flowering plants, including orchids, gentians, sea lavender, honeysuckle, wild gladioli, crown daisies, prickly pear, buttercups, clematis, poppies, and pink convolvulus.

SEARCHING FOR ATLANTIS

In 2011, a team of archaeologists studying at Doñana National Park claimed they had found the location of the fabled lost city of Atlantis in a marshy area at the center of the park. Atlantis is a legendary city that is said to have sunk into the sea, although no one is really sure if the city ever existed. The scientists analyzed satellite imagery of what looked like a sunken city and then went to the site and used ground radar and digital mapping to survey the site more closely. They believe they have found concentric rings of structures that may be the remains of Atlantis. The team plans to excavate further at the site.

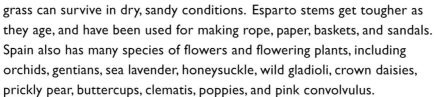

The central Pyrenees feature vast pine forests.

LAND IN DANGER

Spain is contending with numerous environmental issues. The dumping of raw sewage and the byproducts of offshore oil and gasoline production have polluted the Mediterranean Sea. Air pollution is a problem in Spain as it is in many industrialized countries. European environmental authorities have noted that air pollution levels have recently exceeded recommended levels in Spain's large cities.

The land itself has also suffered, as deforestation for construction and land clearing has resulted in a loss of topsoil. This loss, in turn, leads to desertification, making the land barren and no longer useful for agriculture. Approximately one-third of Spain's land is threatened by desertification, not only from deforestation, but also as a result of drought, forest fires, overgrazing, and bad farming practices.[4]

The Spanish government has taken steps to protect the nation's ecosystems, establishing 14 national parks covering almost 1,300 square miles

UNESCO SITES

The Ordesa y Monte Perdido National Park, located around Mount Perdido, and Doñana National Park, located on the coast of the Andalusia region, are both UNESCO World Heritage Sites. UNESCO stands for the United Nations Educational, Scientific and Cultural Organization. UNESCO has designated World Heritage Sites all over the world. These are sites that are considered to be part of the cultural and natural heritage of the entire world, and as such are given special protection.

Lake Ercina, located in one of Spain's national parks, is a popular hiking spot.

(3,400 sq km) of land.[5] These parks are found throughout the country, and protect diverse landscapes. Within their boundaries are mountains, wetlands, beaches, forests, and lakes. National parks in the Canary Islands feature volcanoes, craters, and solidified lava flows. Other parks are habitats for rare and endangered species of animals and birds.

CHAPTER 4

HISTORY: FROM EMPIRES TO A REPUBLIC

Stone tools discovered by archaeologists point to the presence of hominids in Spain as early as 1 million years ago. The earliest evidence of modern humans dates to approximately 35,000 years ago. These people left behind sophisticated paintings and carvings in caves which dot the Cantabrian Mountains in northern Spain. After 3200 BCE, larger settlements began forming as technology improved at a rapid pace. The coming of copper tools, complex fortifications, and advances in agriculture made these communities possible.

The Bronze Age, beginning around 2000 BCE, saw the movement of settlements to more easily defensible areas. Social stratification, the separation of people into different social classes, has been observed by

Cave paintings in Spain have been found to be 30,000 or more years old.

archaeologists. Some ancient individuals are buried with jewelry, while others are buried with swords or pottery. Settlers moved throughout the Iberian Peninsula during this era, establishing villages and farms.

The Phoenicians, a civilization based in the eastern area of the Mediterranean, traveled to Spain by 800 BCE. They established settlements after discovering deposits of silver, gold, and tin in southern Spain. The Greeks traveled to the Iberian Peninsula by the seventh century BCE, trading olive oil, pottery, and other goods. The indigenous Iberian societies began adopting the culture and technologies of the Phoenicians and Greeks, even developing writing systems based on their languages. Largely insulated from these developments were the Celtic people living further inland. These central European people, who had settled in the

ALTAMIRA CAVE

Altamira Cave, in northern Spain, preserves the nation's most famous cave paintings. Dating from tens of thousands of years ago, the images were painted with pigments from locally found stones and minerals mixed with animal fat. They depict animals that would have been used for food, such as horses, bison, red deer, and reindeer. Archaeologists are unsure why the pictures were painted, but theorize they could be religious decorations or part of initiation rites for young hunters.

A museum outside Altamira Cave holds replicas of the cave's paintings.

Iberian Peninsula by the sixth century BCE, split into numerous different tribes and territories and became skilled in metalworking and pottery.

THE ROMANS

Carthage, a powerful city-state based in North Africa that was once a Phoenician colony, conquered much of Spain in the third century BCE. Disputes between the Roman Empire and Carthage led to a series of wars known as the Punic Wars. During the Second Punic War (218–201 BCE), Carthaginian forces in Spain were soundly defeated by the Roman military, resulting in Roman control over much of the southern Iberian Peninsula by 206 BCE. In the subsequent decades, Roman forces trying to expand their control over more of the peninsula fought against various groups of Celts and indigenous Iberians. Roman Spain steadily but slowly increased in size through these conflicts.

Controlling the Iberian Peninsula provided Rome with secure sea routes to Great Britain, western Gaul (modern-day France), and the mouth of the Rhine River. The empire also benefited from taxes imposed on the Spanish people and the natural resources available on the peninsula. One especially breathtaking artifact of this era, still visible today, is the Roman gold mine at Las Médulas.

The Roman town of Italica, near present-day Seville, is the largest collection of Roman ruins in Spain.

The Roman gold mine at Las Médulas features striking hills and preserved aqueducts and inscriptions.

The legacy of Roman Spain can also be seen in a number of other Roman archaeological sites, and many Roman structures such as aqueducts are still visible today.

As the Roman Empire faded, another invading group entered the Iberian Peninsula in the fourth century, launching a new period in Spanish history. The Visigoths, a group from Eastern Europe, had already adopted some elements of Roman culture. When they entered Spain around 376 CE, their culture was a mixture of German and Roman customs. They ruled over much of the peninsula, but a few small kingdoms remained independent. The seventh century brought advances in Visigoth law and culture, but by the dawn of the eighth century, government infighting and religious disputes had left the Visigoths weakened.

The Visigoths managed to capture the city of Rome itself in 410.

MUSLIM SPAIN

By 700, Muslim armies had conquered much of North Africa, the inhabitants of which were known as the Moors. In July 710, a group of 400 Muslim soldiers crossed into Spain from North Africa through the Strait of Gibraltar.[1] They were a reconnaissance force, sent to see if anyone would challenge them. They met little resistance. The next

A group of Moorish princes controlled parts of Spain for hundreds of years.

spring, a Moorish army of 7,000 men led by Tariq ibn Ziyad crossed the strait again and established a camp at the base of the Rock of Gibraltar, which they called Jabal Tariq, or "Hill of Tariq."[2] Some historians believe the army had actually been invited to participate in Visigoth infighting. In any event, for the next several hundred years, the Muslim Moors controlled various parts of Spain. Their culture would influence Spain for even longer.

The Muslim forces conquered Spain city by city. They gave the inhabitants the option of converting to Islam but did not force them to do so. Those who declined to convert were subject to special taxes, and were generally treated as second-class citizens. As with Christian Spain, the economy in Muslim Spain was based largely on agriculture and livestock, with less emphasis on industry. The Moors developed a rich cultural tradition, making lasting contributions to literature, poetry, philosophy, and astronomy. Important technologies developed by the Moors in Spain included windmills, paper manufacturing, and irrigation systems.

The Iberian people often rebelled against their Muslim rulers. Bit by bit, the Iberians regained their land from Muslim control over a 700-year period known as the Reconquista, and by 1249 only the kingdom of Granada remained in Moorish hands. As they regained territory, the Spanish formed new Christian kingdoms. Queen Isabella of Castile and

The Moors surrender Granada to Queen Isabella and King Ferdinand.

King Ferdinand of Aragon married in 1469 and would rule all of Spain as powerful partners for many years.

RELIGIOUS INTOLERANCE

Spain flourished under Ferdinand and Isabella. They established an extensive trading network. Spanish traders purchased goods from Africa and Asia and sold them in Europe.

However, the relative religious tolerance promoted by the Moors quickly came to an end. Ferdinand and Isabella formed a new institution called the Spanish Inquisition in 1480 to interrogate converts to Christianity and investigate accusations of heresy. The inquisition often used torture methods against the people it interrogated. The Reconquista finally ended in 1492, when Granada was reclaimed by Ferdinand and Isabella. That same year, a royal decree ordered all Spanish Jews to either convert or be expelled from the country, and in 1501 a similar decree applied to Spanish Muslims.

Also in 1492, Isabella and Ferdinand agreed to finance the voyage of Christopher Columbus, who launched the first of many expeditions to the Americas. The conquests of Columbus and the Spanish explorers

Ferdinand and Isabella became king and queen at ages 22 and 23, respectively.

Spanish explorers sailed to the Americas in ships like this replica of Columbus's *Santa Maria*.

that followed him created a Spanish empire rich with treasures from the Americas.

In 1588, Spain's King Philip II sent a fleet called the Spanish Armada to conquer England. Because of bad weather, poor decisions, and a lack of supplies, the Armada was defeated by the British Navy. Soon Spain had lost territories it held in Europe, and France controlled some formerly Spanish lands. The War of the Spanish Succession (1701–1714) began when King Charles II of Spain died without an heir and France's King Louis XIV declared his grandson king. The new king, Philip V, belonged to the House of Bourbon. Great Britain, Portugal, and the Holy Roman Empire were threatened by the prospect of a powerful, unified Spanish and French empire. The Spanish people were split, with some in favor of such a union and some opposed. The war, fought in Europe and North America, would eventually pit Spain and France against Spaniards

SPANISH EXPLORERS

Some of the most famous Spanish explorers include: Hernán Cortés, who conquered the Aztec Empire in Mexico; Francisco Pizarro, who conquered the Incan Empire of western South America; Juan Ponce de León, who explored what is now the state of Florida; and Hernando de Soto, Álvar Núñez Cabeza de Vaca, and Francisco Vásquez de Coronado, the first Europeans to explore what is now the southern United States.

The Spanish Armada was soundly defeated by the British Navy in 1588.

loyal to the previous regime, Great Britain, and Portugal, among others. The series of treaties that ended the war resulted in Spain losing most of its territorial possessions in Europe beyond its own borders, including Gibraltar and Sicily.

FROM THE PENINSULAR WAR TO CIVIL WAR

In 1807, a combined force of Spanish and French armies invaded Portugal. The next year, France attacked its ally Spain, launching the Peninsular War (1808–1814). Though the Spanish armies were relatively weak compared to those of France, they were aided by both the British military and a new tactic known as guerilla warfare. Spanish guerillas did not wear military uniforms, and rather than meeting the enemy army in massed groups, they engaged in small raids and ambushes to gradually weaken the French. In 1812, a new constitution inspired by that of Revolutionary France was established. Spain now had a limited monarchy, a parliament, and a modern system of administration.

Though Spain won the war, continuous fighting broke out between those who supported the new constitution and those who supported an absolute monarch. Three Carlist Wars—named for Carlos V, who attempted to claim the Spanish throne—were fought beginning in the 1830s between the forces of traditional Catholicism and supporters of liberalism. The unrest continued into the 1870s as Spain went through

The French Army, *right*, surrenders to the Spanish Army at the Battle of Balíen during the Peninsular War.

military revolts, the exile and return of the monarchy, and a brief period of time as a republic. Finally, in 1875, a peace settlement led to the restoration of the monarchy, and a period of relative stability followed.

From April to August 1898, Spain fought the Spanish-American War with the United States over its last foreign colonies, Cuba and the Philippines. The war had begun in 1895 as the Cuban War of Independence (1895–1898). After losing the Spanish-American War, Spain lost these colonies. Spain remained neutral during World War I (1914–1918), with no military involvement.

Though it was neutral, Spain still lost shipping vessels to German submarines during World War I.

In 1923, King Alfonso XIII was ruling Spain when a general named Miguel Primo de Riviera led a revolution against the unstable government. The king, knowing he had no choice against the power of the people and the military, supported this coup and Primo de Riviera became the prime minister. However, he effectively became a dictator. His rule only lasted until 1930, when economic troubles resulted in a decline in his popularity and both the military and the king turned against him. In 1931, Spain held municipal elections, and the people voted overwhelmingly for the Republican and Socialist parties. Fearing civil war or revolution, Alfonso left the country. Many believed they had enacted a peaceful revolution without any bloodshed.

The landing of American troops in Cuba marked the beginning of the end of Spain's control over its last foreign colonies.

But the new republic did not last. Inequality still reigned in Spain, and many political parties fought for power. In 1936, a general in the Spanish Army named Francisco Franco initiated the Spanish Civil War (1936–1939). Franco was supported by the Francoists, Spaniards who believed in a government ruled by one person. He also received help from Italy's dictator Benito Mussolini and Germany's Adolf Hitler. Aligned against these forces were the Republicans, who fought for democracy. After three years, Franco's side won, at a cost of more than 500,000 lives.[3]

Many international fighters, including British writer George Orwell, traveled to Spain to aid the Republicans.

During World War II (1939–1945), Spain described itself as nonbelligerent rather than neutral. While the nation did not want to officially enter the war, it did provide support to the Axis powers of Italy and Germany. This included material and economic assistance. Additionally, Spanish volunteers fought for the Axis forces. Following the Axis defeat, the victorious powers, including the United States, the United Kingdom, and the Soviet Union, isolated Spain in retaliation for its support for the Axis. Franco's Spain was not admitted to the United Nations (UN) until 1955, ten years after the war.

Franco, known as Generalisimo, or supreme commander, ruled Spain for almost 40 years until his death in 1975. Though he oversaw economic growth, he was essentially a dictator who held all governmental power

Francisco Franco, *right*, meets with Adolf Hitler in 1940.

and forcibly silenced critics. He even appointed the man who would succeed him, Juan Carlos I, in an attempt to restore the monarchy to Spain. Juan Carlos was the grandson of the last Spanish king, Alfonso XIII.

However, Juan Carlos I did not follow Franco's example. In 1977, he allowed Spain's first free elections in 41 years. A democratic government was established, and by 1978 Spain had a new constitution and formally became a parliamentary monarchy.

Under the new government, Spain strengthened ties with other modern nations. In 1982, Spain joined the North Atlantic Treaty Organization (NATO), and in 1986 it joined the European Union (EU). Today, Spain is a vibrant part of modern Europe, enjoying a rich culture owed to a long history interwoven by many different peoples and cultures.

NATO

The North Atlantic Treaty Organization (NATO) is a group of countries that have signed a treaty pledging to defend each other against any attack by an external party. As of 2012, 28 countries belonged to NATO.[4]

Juan Carlos I with his wife on a 1997 visit to Germany

CHAPTER 5

PEOPLE: UNITED DIVERSITY

The Spanish people have a mixture of Mediterranean and northern European Nordic ancestry, resulting from the invasions and immigrations that brought a variety of people to the country throughout its history. The Celts and the Visigoths contributed Nordic heritage, while the Moors and the Romans contributed their Mediterranean heritage. Present-day immigration continues to add to the nation's diversity.

15.1 percent of Spain's population is under the age of 15.

LANGUAGE

Because of their strong ties to their individual regions, not all Spaniards speak the country's official language of Castilian

Fans in Madrid react after Spain scores a goal in the 2010 World Cup. Passion for soccer helps to unify Spain's diverse population.

YOU SAY IT!

English	Spanish
Hello	Hola (OH-la)
How are you?	¿Cómo estás? (KOH-moh ehs-TAHS?)
Fine, thank you	Muy bien, gracias (MOO-ee byehn, GRAH-syahs)
Thank you (very much)	(Muchas) gracias (MOO-chas GRAH-syahs)
You're welcome	De nada (DAY NAH-da)
Good-bye	Adiós (ah-DYOS)
Welcome	Bienvenido (BIEN-ven-eedo)

Spanish. Only 74 percent of the country speaks it as their primary language.[1] The Catalan language, spoken by 17 percent of the population, is the official language in the Catalonia region, as well as the Balearic Islands and Valencia, where it is called Valencian rather than Catalan.[2] In the northwest corner of Catalonia, Aranese and Catalan are both official languages. Many who live in the Basque country speak the Basque language, and Galician is the official language in Galicia. Basque and Galician are spoken by 2 percent and 7 percent of Spaniards, respectively.[3]

This assortment of official languages underlines the independence of each region of Spain and the determination of each to preserve its unique identity. However, official Castilian Spanish is understood everywhere, and many people speak English as well. In the 1978 Constitution, Castilian Spanish is designated as the official language of the entire country, but other languages are permitted to be co-official in certain regions.

SPANISH SURNAMES

Spanish naming traditions dictate that Spanish women do not change their surnames when they get married. Instead, a woman keeps her name, and her children are given both her first surname and that of their father. For example, if a woman named Esmerelda Pérez Rodriguez marries a man named Juan García Martínez, her name remains the same and her children's surname is García Pérez.

Castilian Spanish began as a dialect spoken in northern Spain, but by the twelfth century it was the language spoken in the royal courts of Castile and León. When Ferdinand and Isabella united their kingdoms and began ruling Spain, Castilian became the official state language. Similar to many other European Romance languages, its roots are in Latin, but throughout its history Castilian has also adopted words from other languages, including Arabic words introduced during the Moorish occupation of Spain.

THE UNOFFICIAL OFFICIAL RELIGION

The Spanish people are heavily Roman Catholic, with 94 percent adhering to that religion.[4] Roman Catholicism was the official state religion from the Civil War until 1978, when Spain's constitution went into effect. Spain now proclaims no official religion, but the government still provides some financial support to the Catholic Church. Only approximately 21 percent of Spaniards report regularly going to church.[5] For most people, religion mostly enters their lives through formal occasions such as marriages, funerals, and festivals. However, many of Spain's customs have their roots in traditional Catholicism.

Catholicism first became the official religion of Spain in 589.

Spanish Catholics attend mass in Catalonia.

While only 6 percent of Spaniards are not Roman Catholics, there is a rapidly growing population of Muslims as a result of immigration from Islamic countries.[6] Though there are also a handful of adherents to Judaism, Spain's history of persecuting or exiling Jews diminished their numbers during medieval times and the population never recovered.

SIESTA

Traditionally, in the Spanish lifestyle, the midday meal was always followed by a nap called a siesta, taken during the hottest part of the day. People did not return to work for several hours, and then stayed out and ate their evening meal late. However, now that many people commute long distances from home to work it is no longer practical to return home for several hours in the middle of the day for a siesta, and the custom is declining.

LIVING IN SPAIN

In 2012, Spain had a population of 47,042,984, making it the twenty-seventh most populous country in the world.[7] More than three-quarters of the population lived in cities, with Madrid, Barcelona, and Valencia being the most populated.[8] The median age was 40.9 years, and the average life expectancy was 81.27 years.[9]

Spanish households are frequently multigenerational.

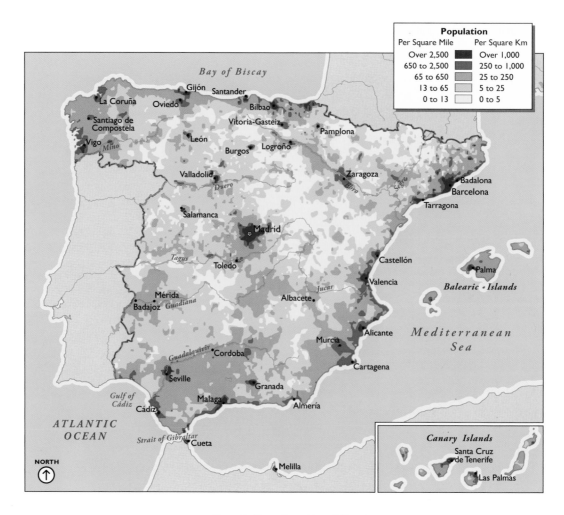

Population

Per Square Mile		Per Square Km
Over 2,500		Over 1,000
650 to 2,500		250 to 1,000
65 to 650		25 to 250
13 to 65		5 to 25
0 to 13		0 to 5

Bay of Biscay

La Coruña
Gijón   Santander
Oviedo   Bilbao
Santiago de Compostela   Vitoria-Gasteiz
Vigo   Mino   Pamplona
León
Burgos   Logroño
Valladolid   Zaragoza
Duero   Ebro   Badalona
Segre   Barcelona
Salamanca   Tarragona
Madrid
Tagus   Castellón
Toledo   Jucar   Valencia
Mérida   Guadiana   Albacete   Balearic · Islands
Badajoz   Palma
Murcia   Alicante   Mediterranean
Guadalquivir   Cordoba   Sea
Cartagena
Seville
Granada
Gulf of   Malaga
Cádiz   Cádiz   Almería
ATLANTIC
OCEAN
Strait of Gibraltar   Cueta

NORTH
↑

Melilla

Canary Islands
Santa Cruz de Tenerife
Las Palmas

Population Density of Spain

In Spain, families tend to be tight-knit. Large families will often live together, and many working women rely on their parents for child care. Women have found some degree of equality only in the years since Franco's death. Before that time, women's lives were bound by a strict code of conduct, mostly laid out by the moral code of the Catholic Church. Under Spanish law, women needed their husband's permission to do anything, including getting a job, buying property, and traveling away from their homes.

Once democracy was established in Spain, women's status changed dramatically. They no longer needed their husband's permission to do basic things, and soon contraceptives, divorce, and abortion were legalized. Adult women increased their university attendance and employment rates. However, these changes also resulted in a drop in Spain's birth rate. In 2012, the average woman had 1.48 children.[10]

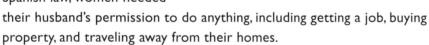

SECOND HOMES

More people in Spain own a second home than in any other EU country. In many cases, this is because people who left their villages to work in large cities never sold their family homes. Most people who live in the city live in high-rise apartments, returning to their family homes on weekends and for vacations.

Approximately one-sixth of Spaniards are 65 or older.

As with many modern countries, Spain is finding it has to adjust to modern life in ways that do not necessarily follow its traditional family values. Because women have more options and can now work outside the home, and because the marriage rate is low and divorce is easily available, it is not always possible to care for the family's elderly at home. Students who once attended universities near their homes may now travel further for their educations. Nursing homes are now needed for the elderly whose families cannot care for them.

Spain's modernization has meant that many elderly must live either independently or in a nursing home.

CHAPTER 6
CULTURE: BEYOND BULLFIGHTS

Throughout its long and colorful history, Spain has fostered many great artists who are known throughout the world. They include Francisco de Goya, Pablo Picasso, Joan Miró, Salvador Dalí, and Antoni Tàpies. Goya was a Romantic artist and printmaker whose work bridged classical painting and the modern era. His painting *The Third of May 1808* depicts a period when French armies invaded Spain. Goya chronicled and commented on many of the events of his time in his paintings. Picasso was one of the most influential artists of the twentieth century. He worked in a nonrealistic style known as cubism. Miró was a painter and sculptor who also worked with ceramics. His work is in the style of surrealism; he rejected traditional realistic painting styles as too dull. He also saw his art as an expression of his pride in being Catalan. Dalí, another surrealist from Catalan, worked in painting, film, sculpture, and photography. One of his most famous works is called The *Persistence of*

The Prado Museum in Madrid houses an extensive collection of paintings by Goya.

Memory. The oil painting depicts soft, melting pocket watches that can be seen to symbolize the idea that time is not rigid. Tàpies, a painter, sculptor, and art theorist from Barcelona, was known for his abstract expressionist art. This type of art aims to express the artist's feelings rather than present a realistic depiction of something. His paintings often include elements such as clay, marble, rags, waste paper, and string.

Spain is also known for its handcrafted products, including guitars, lace, pottery, ceramics, and leather. Many of the country's best-known crafts have long histories. Archaeologists have discovered pottery in Spain dating from 6,000 years ago, and an ancestor of the modern guitar, an instrument called the oud, was brought to Spain by the Moors in the eighth century.

Spanish literature is also well known, especially the novel *Don Quixote* by Miguel de Cervantes, first published in 1605. The book tells the story of a man who reads too many novels about chivalrous knights, adopts the name Don Quixote, and decides to strike out on an adventure of his own. A more recent Spanish literary figure is Federico García Lorca, a twentieth century poet and playwright born in 1898. He became notable for his experimental poems and plays, and was a friend and collaborator of Dalí. Lorca was shot and killed by Francoist forces during the Spanish Civil War in 1936. Another famous Spanish writer of novels and short stories, Camilo José Cela, was born in 1916 and remained loyal to Franco during the Spanish Civil War. Later in his career,

A statue of Don Quixote stands in Madrid.

his work became experimental; in 1988, he wrote a novel consisting of a single sentence more than 100 pages long. He won the Nobel Prize in Literature in 1989 and died in 2002. One of the most popular Spanish authors today is Carlos Ruiz Zafón. His novels have been translated into many languages and published in dozens of countries.

MUSIC AND FILM

Spain is also famous for a type of music and dance called flamenco, an important part of many fiestas and celebrations. Some believe flamenco came to Spain with traveling Romani people. These people originally came from northern India

SPANISH ARCHITECTURE

Architecture in Spain mixes European and Arabic influences. Some of the most beautiful buildings in Spain, including the Alhambra Palace in Granada and the Giralda Tower in Seville, demonstrate Arabic design. Others, such as the San Lorenzo de El Escorial monastery outside of Madrid and the Royal Palace of Madrid, reflect European architectural traditions.

Perhaps the most famous modern Spanish architect was Antoni Gaudí, who worked mostly in Barcelona in the late nineteenth and early twentieth century. His work was influenced by nature. His masterpiece is the Sagrada Família, a massive Roman Catholic church in Barcelona. Construction began in 1882, and is not expected to be fully completed until as late as 2028.

Historians believe the origins of flamenco date back as early as the ninth century.

but settled throughout Asia and Europe. At first, flamenco was likely vocal music accompanied only by rhythmic hand clapping. Later, a guitar accompaniment and dancing were introduced, and by 1765 flamenco schools were founded to teach both the music and the dance steps. The golden age of flamenco took place between 1869 and 1910, when the most powerful type of flamenco singing was developed, called *cante jondo*, or "deep song." Soon flamenco was being performed all over the world. Although its popularity has seen ups and downs since then, there are still plenty of small flamenco clubs and professional theatrical concerts where flamenco music and dance are performed.

The *jota* is another kind of Spanish folk music. It includes a dance performed in regional costume, often accompanied by castanets. Classical composers such as Bizet and Liszt incorporated the musical form into some of their works. The *sardana*, another folk dance, is performed in a circle and accompanied by a band called a *cobla*, consisting of wind, brass, and stringed instruments as well as a drum.

Spain is also the birthplace of two world-renowned musicians. Guitarist Andrés Segovia is one of the best-known and most influential classical guitar players of the twentieth century. He is renowned for his ability to take classical music written for other instruments and transcribe it for the guitar. Opera singer and conductor Plácido Domingo, born in 1941, is known for his beautiful tenor voice. He has performed more tenor opera roles than any other tenor singer in history.[1]

Spain's pop music industry has been active since Franco's death, and developments in the 1980s helped make the nation's music uniquely

Plácido Domingo sings in Chile in 2007.

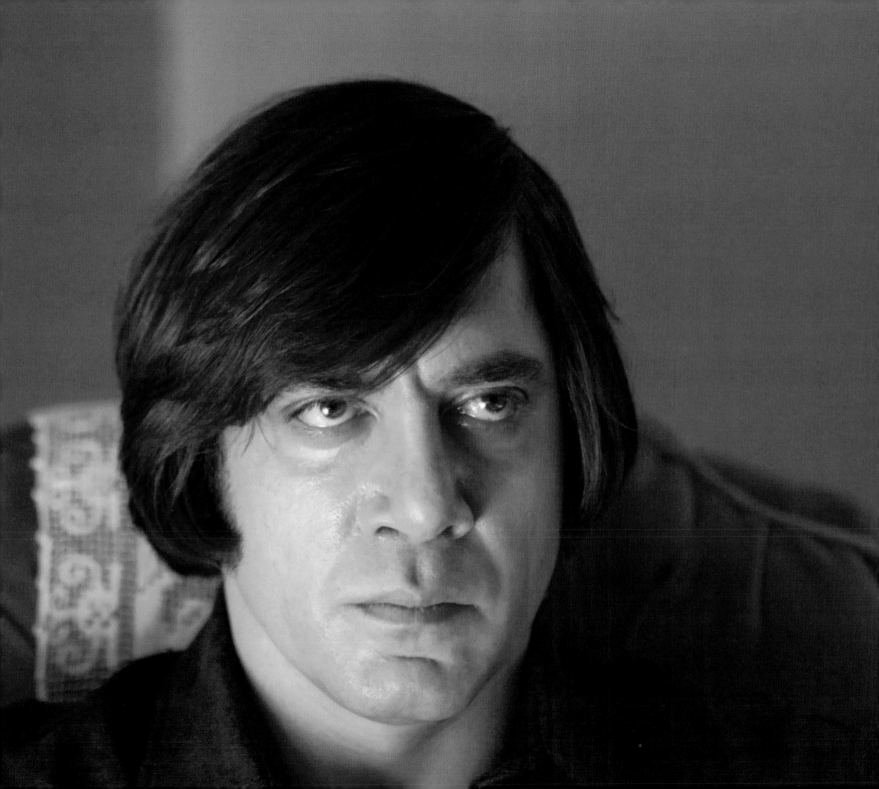

Spanish. Though Spanish pop music once relied on American and British influences for its style, it now stands apart. Popular genres include blues, hip-hop, rock, and Latin rhythm. Julio Iglesias and his son Enrique Iglesias are two of the most internationally successful Spanish singers of all time.

Though most of the popular films shown in Spanish movie houses are from the United States or elsewhere in Europe, Spain does have a small homegrown film industry. Landmark director Luis Buñuel, a friend of Dalí, was forced to leave Spain during much of Franco's regime. As a result, most of his films were shot outside of Spain.

Later Spanish filmmakers generally did not find much success outside their home country, though Spanish director Pedro Almodóvar's 1999 comedy *All About My Mother* did win the Academy Award for Best Foreign Language Film, and director Alejandro Amenábar won the same award for *Mar adentro* (*The Sea Inside*) in 2005. Actor Javier Bardem won the Academy Award for Best Supporting Actor in 2008 for his chilling portrayal of assassin Anton Chigurh in *No Country for Old Men*.

TIME TO CELEBRATE

Spain's cultural heritage is visible in the holidays and festivals the nation celebrates. Many of these festivals are based on religious occasions,

Spanish actor Javier Bardem in *No Country for Old Men*

although the religious aspects have become less important in recent years. Some holidays are celebrated nationally, while others relate to a specific region or community. National holidays include Spanish National Day on October 12 and Day of the Constitution on December 6. Traditional holidays include Christmas and Saint Joseph's Day, celebrated on March 19. Carnavále and Easter are other major celebrations.

Another Spanish holiday is the Festival of San Fermín, when the running of the bulls takes place in Pamplona in northern Spain. Beginning on July 7, the bulls to be used in the bullfighting arena are released to run through the streets of the town. Locals and tourists alike run ahead of the bulls, wearing special white shirts and red sashes. The event dates to the thirteenth century, and was originally a way to move the animals from their holding pens to the bullfighting ring.

TIÓ DE NADAL

In Catalonia, children traditionally receive gifts on December 24 from a wooden log named Tió de Nadal. The children decorate the log, then leave the room to say a prayer and sing a song to El Tió. When they come back, it is covered by a cloth. They tap Tió de Nadal with a stick and then lift the cloth to find presents underneath it.

SPANISH FOOD

As with most everything about Spain, food varies widely from region to region. Staple foods in Spain include pork, chicken, beef, fish, seafood, lentils, and chickpeas. Garlic and olive

A wide variety of cured meats are popular in Spain.

oil are used frequently, and popular spices include paprika, tarragon, and saffron. Seafood is especially popular along the coasts, with meat more frequently served in the inland regions. One of Spain's most famous dishes is paella, a mixture of rice flavored with saffron served with vegetables, seafood, and meat or chicken. Gazpacho, a spicy, tomato-based raw vegetable soup served cold, is another famous Spanish dish.

Another popular item on Spanish menus is cured meat, usually pork based. This traditional food, which dates back to the Roman occupation of the Iberian Peninsula, includes several variations differentiated by the length of the aging processes and the selection of spices used. Some styles are cured for up to four years.

Many Spaniards drink strong coffee, either espresso or coffee laced with alcohol. Children often drink thick hot chocolate. Adults also enjoy sangría, a drink made from wine, brandy, and chopped fruit.

Spain is among the world's largest wine-producing countries.

BULLFIGHTING AND SPORTS

Among the best-known Spanish traditions is bullfighting. Part of many of the country's fiestas, bullfighting likely had its start in the Middle Ages as a sport for the aristocratic class, who fought bulls from horseback as part of their military training. By the eighteenth century, people who were too poor to own horses had invented a version that could be done on foot.

Bullfighting today follows a very specific order. There are three matadors, or bullfighters, each with his own team, and each matador follows specific steps in the arena. First, the matador shows off his skill

Bullfighting, the ritual killing of bulls, is a controversial Spanish tradition.

BULLFIGHTING BREEDS

Bullfighting might not be possible without a very special breed of bull called the *toro bravo* or *toro de lidia*, now found only in Spain. These bulls once ran wild on the plains and were bred for aggression, energy, stamina, and strength. They may have first been used for arena games during the Roman Empire. Through DNA studies, scientists have discovered these bulls are related to African cattle, suggesting they may originally have come from North Africa.

by facing the bull with only his cape. Next, he is joined by the picadors, who are on horseback and use lances to harass the bull. Then three more team members, the banderilleros, each stick a pair of short spears into the bull's back. Then the matador steps in again and uses his red cape to entice the bull. The bullfight ends when he kills the bull with his sword. After the fight, the carcass is processed and the meat sold.

Bullfighting is both defended and criticized passionately in Spain. Animal rights activists decry the killing of bulls for entertainment, while defenders see it as a source of employment, a long-standing tradition, and even a form of Spanish art. Some Spanish regions have banned the practice of bullfighting. The Canary Islands became the first of these in 1991, and a ban in Catalonia took effect on January 1, 2012.

Like most European countries, soccer is also very important. Spain's national soccer team saw great success in the early twenty-first

José Calderón makes a play during a 2012 Olympic match against Great Britain.

century, with victories in the 2008 and 2012 European Championships, as well as in the 2010 World Cup. Tennis, bicycling, and motorcycling have become popular pursuits as well. Spaniards also enjoy basketball,

and several Spanish players now play professional basketball in the United States, including José Calderón and Ricky Rubio. The Spanish basketball team won the silver medal at the 2012 Summer Olympics in London. Jai alai, based on the Basque game pelota, is a popular sport in the Basque region. It involves bouncing a ball off a walled court, using a basket-like scoop instead of a racket. Jai alai has become popular in parts of the United States as well.

The ball in jai alai can move at speeds exceeding 180 miles per hour (290 km/h).

Jai alai players must wear protective gear due to the game's high speeds.

CHAPTER 7
POLITICS: A MODERN MONARCHY

A parliamentary monarchy is a system of government where the monarch is more of a figurehead than an actual leader. The monarch does not create or directly implement policies; instead, the real power of the government lies with the prime minster, the cabinet, and a legislature. Many modern monarchies, including the United Kingdom, resemble this basic form. The king of Spain represents unity and permanence for the Spanish people. Since the prime minister and the cabinet are drawn from the popularly elected legislature, the government is more democratic than the presence of a king might lead one to suspect.

The implementation of a new constitution in 1978, overwhelmingly approved by Spanish voters in December of that year, made parliamentary monarchy the official form of government in Spain. Although some rebel groups attempted to reinstate military-controlled governments over

The parliament building in Madrid sits near the city's center.

THE SPANISH FLAG

The Spanish flag depicts a wide yellow horizontal stripe at its center along with thinner red horizontal stripes on the top and bottom. On the left side, within the yellow stripe, Spain's coat of arms appears. The coat of arms features the emblems of Spain's traditional kingdoms, and is flanked by pillars representing the Pillars of Hercules. The flag was adopted in December 1981.

the next few years, King Juan Carlos was able to use his personal authority and his popularity as Spain's official monarch to maintain the newly formed democratic government.

The 1978 constitution formally laid out Spain's most important values: liberty, justice, equality, and the right to hold and espouse differing political views. It established the role of political parties, requiring that these parties follow established democratic procedures. The constitution also set forth the basic rights of Spanish citizens, declaring that all are equal before the law regardless of age, gender, race, or religion.

The constitution also deliberately reduces the influence and power of two institutions that historically possessed a great deal of power in Spain: the armed forces and the Catholic Church. The constitution clearly defines and limits the roles of both. While the armed forces are tasked

Spain's flag

with protecting Spain and its independence, the constitution emphasizes that ultimately the government of Spain, not the military, is responsible for defending the country. Where religion is concerned, the constitution defends the right of individuals to religious freedom and states there will be no official state religion. It avoids cutting all ties with traditional religious authorities, however, guaranteeing the government will maintain good relations with the Catholic Church and take into account the religious beliefs of Spanish citizens when necessary.

RUNNING THEIR OWN REGION

Perhaps the biggest change outlined in the constitution is the fact that a large degree of autonomy was granted to the regions of Spain. The seventeen autonomous communities and two autonomous cities of Spain have the power to do a great deal of self-governing. During the first five years following the implementation of the 1978 constitution, the central Spanish government gave the regions control of matters such as urban planning, public works, health and welfare, and environmental protection. They were also permitted to control sports, leisure activities, and tourism in their regions.

The transition to autonomous control by the individual regions has not been easy. There are often disputes between regions and the central Spanish government, especially when it comes to making it clear who has which powers and who pays for what. Some of Spain's regions, including the Basque and Catalan regions, are especially strong and determined to retain as much regional control as possible.

HOW IT WORKS

Spain's government operates with the king as the head of state. The prime minister is the head of government. The prime minister and his or her cabinet of advisers, also called the Council of Ministers, are appointed by the monarch in consultation with the legislature. The legislature, known as the National Assembly, is bicameral, meaning it contains two separate legislative bodies. These are the Congress of Deputies, containing 350 members, and the Senate, containing 266 members. Deputies are elected by a proportional party system. Spaniards vote for political parties, and each party is given a number of seats in proportion with the election results. The parties choose the deputies to fill these seats. Senators are elected in each of Spain's regions and subregions,

STRUCTURE OF THE GOVERNMENT OF SPAIN

Executive Branch	Legislative Branch	Judicial Branch
King Prime Minister Council of Ministers	Congress of Deputies Senate	Tribunal Supremo Constitutional Court

including the island areas and the North African cities of Ceuta and Melilla. Regions are given extra senators based on the size of their population. All legislative members serve four-year terms.

In addition to the National Assembly, the prime minister, the Council of Ministers, and the king, there is also a Council of State, a team of advisers to the government. However, their recommendations are nonbinding, which means they can advise the government but the government is not required to take their advice.

Spain's justice system includes the Tribunal Supremo, or "Supreme Court," as the highest legal court in the country. The court consists of five separate chambers, each

EARLY STRUGGLES

As with many aspects of government, Spain struggled to establish its court system after the new constitution took effect in 1978. The constitution provided for free public defenders and prosecutors for those citizens who could not afford their own lawyers. But in the 1980s, the legal system suffered because there was a severe shortage of money, making it impossible to keep up with a growing caseload in the court systems. This led to both long delays in resolving court cases and corrupt practices, such as lawyers bribing court administrators in order to get their clients' cases heard more quickly.

Prime Minister Mariano Rajoy spoke to the media on the subject of international relations in February 2012.

King Juan Carlos officially opens the proceedings of the Congress of Deputies.

handling a separate area of law. Judges are appointed for life, though they are required to retire at age 70.

The General Council of the Judiciary appoints judges and makes sure ethical standards are followed in the legal system. Ten of the council members are selected for five-year terms by the Congress of Deputies, with the other ten chosen by the Senate.

Constitutional law questions are decided by a special Constitutional Court of 12 judges who serve nine-year terms. Chosen by several different groups and organizations, each judge is required by constitutional law to stop engaging in any other types of political, professional, or commercial activity once appointed to the court in order to avoid any conflict of interest in deciding legal matters. The Constitutional Court is able to overrule decisions made by the Tribunal Supremo.

There is also a National Court, the Audencia Nacional, which handles criminal, administrative, and labor matters throughout Spain. The autonomous communities also have their own court systems; below, at the lowest level, are local courts.

PARTIES AND LEADERS

Two major parties dominate Spanish politics: the Partido Socialista Obrero Español (PSOE), or the Spanish Socialist Workers' Party, and the Partido Popular (PP), or the People's Party. The PSOE, a social-democratic party, was outlawed when Franco was in power. It is often aligned with the labor movement. The PP is a conservative party stemming from a movement formed by Franco loyalists in 1976. Its ideology includes Spanish nationalism, and the party tends to oppose government action in the economy.

OTHER PARTIES

Spain has many different political parties on both the national and regional level. Besides the PSOE and PP, the most successful is Izquierda Unida, or "United Left." Two very powerful regional parties are the Convergència i Unió, or "Convergence and Union," in Catalonia, and the Partido Nacionalista Vasco, or "Basque Nationalist Party," in the Basque region. Spanish electoral laws have resulted in regional parties having significant influence in national politics.

SPANISH TERRORISM

One of the biggest issues the Spanish government has been coping with is a terrorist group known as the Euskadi Ta Askatasuna (ETA), or Basque Fatherland and Liberty, which was founded in 1959 to promote Basque's independence as its own country. The ETA specifically targets Spanish security forces, members of the military, government officials, politicians, and generally anyone who does not support its cause. This group has been responsible for several bombings, and the government of Spain believes it has been responsible for more than 800 deaths.[2] Police work and the aid of France have brought about the virtual defeat of the ETA.

Like many modern nations, Spain has also struggled with international terrorist groups. Radical Islamic terrorists, including al-Qaeda and Pakistani groups sympathetic to them, are known to operate several groups in Spain. A 2004 bombing attack attributed to Islamic fundamentalists took place on commuter trains in Madrid, killing 191 people and wounding more than 1,800.[3]

Juan Carlos I remains the king of Spain. His heir apparent is his son Felipe, born in 1968. Prime Minister Mariano Rajoy assumed office on December 21, 2011. A member of the PP, Rajoy has been involved in politics since 1981. In the 2011 general election, the PP won 44.62 percent of the vote, with the PSOE capturing just 28.73 percent.[1]

In 2005, the chief justice of Spain's Tribunal Supremo, *left*, gave a speech as King Carlos sat nearby.

CHAPTER 8

ECONOMICS: MONEY TROUBLES

Spain's economy is among the largest in the world, and its standard of living is approximately the same as in France and Germany, two other countries in the EU. However, after 15 years of economic growth, Spain was hit by the same economic downturn in 2007 that has affected most other EU countries as well as the United States.

In 2007, Spain's unemployment rate hovered around 8 percent.[1] By the end of 2011, it was over 23 percent.[2] Contributing to the problem was the construction industry, with too many new homes being built and not enough people to buy them. In addition, many Spaniards had purchased houses when lending rates were extremely low, but then were unable to keep paying their mortgages when rates rose or they lost their jobs. The Spanish government attempted to boost the economy by spending money to stimulate economic growth and extending

Spaniards line up outside an unemployment office in December 2011.

unemployment benefits. These efforts stopped neither unemployment from growing nor consumers from spending less. In 2012, Spain was still stuck in an economic downturn, one of several EU countries with continuing economic difficulties. In June 2012, Spain's credit rating was downgraded due to a budget deficit and its inability to restructure its banking system. The downgrade makes it more difficult and more expensive for Spain to borrow money and indicates investors' lowered confidence in the Spanish economy.

INDUSTRIES AND RESOURCES

Spain's major industries include both modern products and agriculture. Its industries include textiles, chemicals, shipbuilding, automobiles, machinery, clothing and footwear, and metals and metal manufacturing. Spaniards also manufacture medical equipment and pharmaceuticals. Spain produces many foods and beverages, including grains, vegetables, olives, meats, fish, grapes, sugar beets, citrus fruit, and dairy products. Tourism is also a huge industry for Spain, with people coming from all over the world to experience its scenery, culture, and food. The country ranks fourth in the world in the number of annual visitors.[3]

Spain's major exports are food, beverages, pharmaceuticals, cars, natural gas, and consumer goods. It is also the third-largest exporter of wine in the world. In March 2012, Spain's exports totaled nearly 20 billion euros, an all-time high.[4]

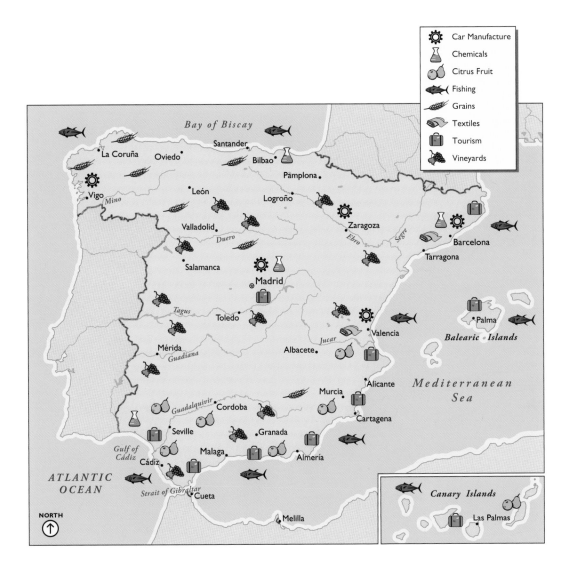

Car Manufacture
Chemicals
Citrus Fruit
Fishing
Grains
Textiles
Tourism
Vineyards

Bay of Biscay

Santander
La Coruña   Oviedo   Bilbao
                                Pamplona
Vigo
    Mino   León   Logroño   Zaragoza
        Valladolid   Barcelona
            Duero   Ebro   Segre   Tarragona
        Salamanca
                    Madrid
        Tagus
            Toledo
    Mérida   Jucar   Valencia   Palma
        Guadiana   Albacete   Balearic Islands
                                    Mediterranean
                    Murcia   Alicante   Sea
    Guadalquivir   Cordoba
        Seville   Granada   Cartagena
Gulf of
Cádiz   Málaga   Almería
    Cádiz
ATLANTIC
OCEAN   Strait of Gibraltar   Cueta
                    Melilla

NORTH
↑

Canary Islands
Las Palmas

Resources of Spain

Like most modern countries, Spain also has to import goods and services that it needs but cannot efficiently produce on its own. Its biggest imports include machinery, fuels, chemicals, food, and medical instruments. In 2011, Spain imported $384 billion worth of goods from other countries. Its major trading partners are Germany, France, Italy, China, the Netherlands, and the United Kingdom.[5]

A CONTAGIOUS ENVIRONMENT

While the EU has created opportunities for its member countries to work together in many ways, it has also created a potentially contagious economic environment. If a country such as Greece has severe money troubles and needs to be bailed out by other EU countries, those economic troubles can begin spreading to other countries as well.

As with many other EU countries, Spain replaced its old currency with the euro in 2002. The country had previously used the Spanish peseta since 1868. Banknotes came in different colors and sizes, and featured portraits of famous Spaniards. The euro banknotes, which replaced the peseta, take a different approach. Since many countries in the EU share the banknotes, they feature examples of architecture rather than portraits of national figures. Banknotes showcase classical,

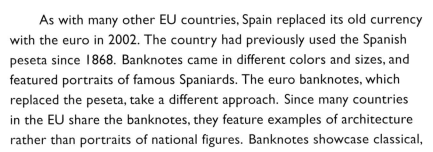

Goods are held at a cargo port in Barcelona, one of the most important trading facilities on the Mediterranean.

Renaissance, and modern architecture, among others. However, euro coins do show national symbols on one side, depending on the country in which they were issued.

WORKING IN SPAIN

Workers in Spain's service industries, such as tourism and health care, made up 71 percent of the workforce in 2011.[6] Another 26 percent work in factories, power plants, or other industrial sites.[7] Since Spain does not have large supplies of raw materials such as minerals, many of the materials needed for manufacturing must be imported, increasing the overall cost of goods and making it more expensive to do business. This often limits the number of workers a company can maintain.

Only approximately 3 percent of Spain's workers are employed

UNEMPLOYMENT STATISTICS

Statistics released by Spain's National Statistics Institute for the year 2011 showed that the country had an extremely high unemployment rate for youth. Approximately 30 percent of those who were unemployed in 2011 were under the age of 30.[8] In addition, 1.6 million Spanish households ended the year in a situation where not a single family member in the household had a job.[9]

In 2012, 17 countries used the euro, including Spain.

A 2011 survey indicated that up to 80 percent of Spain's young people are seriously considering leaving their country to find better jobs and economic opportunities in other places.[12] Not only does this mean Spain could lose most of a generation of young, talented workers with new ideas, but also that there will be fewer young people to fill jobs and buy houses. The real estate market's collapse was one of the reasons why Spain's economy turned sour so quickly. A lack of home buyers may prolong Spain's economic troubles.

in agriculture, including fishing.[10] Since Spain's climate and geography are prone to dry conditions and poor soil, as well as periodic droughts, it is difficult to make a good living from agriculture.

TRYING TO RECOVER

Spain attempted to deal with its economic troubles by implementing austerity measures, under which spending is cut as much as possible. For example, programs related to renewable energy sources, which were once funded by the government, were cut. However, the government's moves were not always well received by Spaniards, who protested against austerity measures—which include pay and benefit cuts—and the rising unemployment rate, which was more than twice the EU average in 2012.[11] Rising unemployment forces the government to pay out more in benefits. It also reduces the

Spanish vineyards supply one of the world's largest wine industries.

amount of money coming into the government because those without an income cannot pay income tax.

The poverty line in Spain is defined as 60 percent of the median income of a household. In 2010, Spain's National Statistics Institute found that 21.8 percent of Spaniards lived below this line, an increase from 17.1 percent in 2009.[13] The problem was even worse for those below 16 years of age. The poverty rate among this group reached 26.5 percent in 2010.[14]

In June 2012, Spain's minister of the economy announced that his country would be seeking economic help from the EU. This economic assistance would be used to add more money to Spain's banks to revitalize the system. Investigators would be looking closely at the banking system before releasing the requested funds. Spain's bank restructuring program, known as Fondo de Reestructuración Ordenada Bancaria, would distribute the funds.

Prime Minister José Luis Rodríguez Zapatero, *right*, met with UN Secretary General Ban Ki Moon in 2011 to discuss solutions to poverty.

CHAPTER 9
SPAIN TODAY

Spaniards once worked from 7:00 or 8:00 a.m. until 1:00 p.m., took a two-hour lunch or siesta break, and then went back to work until as late as 8:00 p.m. With the longer commutes of modern Spaniards, though, those traditions are being dropped. Before, a lunch break might have begun with a snack called a tapa, or appetizer, at a local bar before a worker went home for lunch. Kids in Spain once followed a similar schedule, going to school all morning, going home for lunch, and then returning to school until the late afternoon. Today, they normally have lunch at school. However, the evening meal still often takes place late at night, after 9:00 p.m. People who enjoy nightlife or who like to sit in open-air cafés will sometimes stay out until midnight.

Spanish people do not usually invite people into their homes for socializing if they are not family members. Most socializing, even for teens, takes place outside the home in bars or cafés, and teens may meet

A man sits down to breakfast at a street café in Seville. Breakfast in Spain is typically a small meal.

in a central plaza to hang out together. Even those who stay at home in the evenings may sit outside to enjoy the fresh air.

However, in the winter Spaniards are much more likely to be inside watching television, often for more than three hours a day. Some of the most popular programs include South American soap operas and Spanish situation comedies. News and political shows are also widely viewed. There are two national public television channels, as well as channels in some of the autonomous regions such as Catalonia and Basque. These regional channels broadcast in the local language. As in the United States, there are also several commercial TV channels.

The Spanish people read newspapers, but the practice is not as widespread as in other parts of Europe. This may be because in many Mediterranean countries, citizens tend to rely more on word of mouth and discussions of the daily news, rather than printed newspapers. Newspapers are often available at bars and people read them there. There are many magazines for specific interests such as sports, celebrity gossip, and political issues. Spain boasts a high literacy rate of approximately 98 percent.[1]

EDUCATION IN SPAIN

School in Spain is required until students are 16 years of age. Elementary schoolchildren can attend either public or private schools. Though some

The average Spanish student spends approximately 16 years in school.

private schools receive money from the state, public schools are more strictly controlled by the government. At one time there were two types of public schools, the Bachillerato Unificado Polivalente for students who would be going on to a college or university, and the Formación Profesional for students who would move directly into a manual labor job. However, now all children attend one type of school.

Most children start school at the age of three, even though it is not required until they are six years old. A Spanish elementary school day commonly runs from 9:00 a.m. to 1:00 p.m. and then again from 3:00 p.m. to 5:00 p.m. Afterwards, many kids attend extracurricular activities. Secondary school generally begins at 8:00 a.m. One afternoon a week there are no classes.

There are more students in Spain wishing to attend public colleges than there are places for them, forcing students to compete to get into public universities. This has led some students to travel farther from home in order to get an education. However, as the birthrate in Spain continues to drop, this problem will most likely diminish. Many students must get jobs in order to afford college, although there are more scholarships available now than there once were. Additionally, tuition is generally much lower in Spain than it is in the United States.

Spain spends 4.3 percent of its gross domestic product on education.

College students protest against cuts to education in May 2012.

TEENS IN SPAIN

Similar to teens around the world, Spaniards go to school, hang out with their friends, and have part-time jobs. Summer vacation in Spain runs from mid-June to mid-September, and teens may take vacations with their families, travel, or go to camp.

It was very difficult for teens to find work in Spain in 2012, and their unemployment rate was higher than that of adults. There are strict child labor laws in Spain. The minimum working age in Spain is 16, and teens must seek permission to work from a parent until they are 18.

Spanish teens live in a more permissive culture than those in the United States when it comes to drinking alcohol. As in other European cultures,

THE DRUG TRADE

Despite the increased crackdowns on drug trafficking, one of the major international issues facing Spain is the fact that its long coastline makes it a perfect place for drug shipments to land. Cocaine from Latin America and hashish from North Africa, as well as heroin from Northeast Asia, are routinely unloaded in Spain to be sold to Europeans. Colombian drug traffickers and other organized crime groups also use Spain as a place to launder money, hiding the money's illegal origin from the authorities.

The unemployment rate for Spaniards between the ages of 16 and 24 reached 53 percent in 2012.

many teens are likely to drink wine at home with meals. The drinking age in Spain is 18, but 16-year-olds can buy wine and beer if they have a parent with them. The government claims that 65 percent of 14-to-18-year-olds in Spain drink regularly.[2] However, drinking in public areas is illegal and can lead to fines. Some surveys show that the use of illicit drugs is widespread in Spain, but the same studies also suggest those numbers are falling. Unlike in the United States, possessing and using drugs is not a criminal offense under Spanish law, but taking drugs in public will result in fines.

LOOKING TO THE FUTURE

The Spanish people faced several challenges in 2012. Their most immediate concern was their country's economy. Failing banks, high unemployment, and a downgraded credit rating made it difficult and expensive for Spain to borrow money on the world financial markets. The June 2012 announcement that Spain would be seeking financial aid from other EU members and the enacting of austerity measures showed that Spain hoped to begin turning its economy around.

Like most modern countries, Spain also needs to combat its environmental issues. Many of the government-financed programs designed to help protect the environment have fallen victim to austerity measures. Spain has to contend with pollution in the Mediterranean,

Bicycle exchange programs have been created to reduce pollution from vehicle emissions.

air pollution, deforestation, and desertification. Spain has signed many international environmental treaties, including the Kyoto Protocol in 1998, which restricts greenhouse emissions.

KYOTO PROTOCOL

The Kyoto Protocol is a treaty that was negotiated in the city of Kyoto, Japan, in December 1997 and went into effect on February 16, 2005. The treaty requires its signatories to reduce their greenhouse gas emissions. The United States is one of the few major countries not to ratify the Kyoto Protocol. Canada withdrew from the treaty in December 2011.

Spain is a land steeped in its history but with a firm foundation of family, regional, and national values. It looks to the future with optimism and the knowledge that Spaniards will work to keep their land and people vital and growing for generations to come.

Just as Spain is building the Sagrada Família, it is working to build a brighter future for its people.

TIMELINE

3200 BCE	The first large settlements begin forming in modern-day Spain.
800 BCE	The Phoenicians colonize southern Spain.
206 BCE	The Romans seize the Iberian Peninsula from the Carthaginians.
376 CE	The Visigoths begin settling on the Iberian Peninsula.
711	Moorish armies begin their conquest of Spain.
1249	The Reconquista leaves only Granada in Moorish hands.
1469	Isabella of Castile marries Ferdinand of Aragon.
1480	The Spanish Inquisition begins.
1492	Granada is captured and the Moors are defeated. Christopher Columbus begins his voyages.
1588	King Philip II launches the Spanish Armada in a failed attempt to conquer England.
1701–1714	The War of Spanish Succession is fought, resulting in a Bourbon dynasty takeover of the Spanish throne.
1808–1814	The Peninsular War is fought, leading to a new Spanish Constitution.

1875	The monarchy is restored and a brief period of peace follows.
1898	The Spanish-American War is fought.
1936–1939	Francisco Franco's forces are victorious in the Spanish Civil War and he becomes dictator.
1975	Franco dies and Juan Carlos I is declared king.
1977	King Carlos I establishes political reforms and democratic elections are held.
1978	Spain's new constitution establishes a parliamentary monarchy.
1986	Spain joins the European Union.
1998	Spain signs the Kyoto Protocol.
2002	The Spanish peseta is replaced by the euro.
2004	Extremist Islamic terrorists bomb commuter trains in Madrid, killing 191.
2007	The global economic crisis strikes Spain.
2012	Spain's credit rating is downgraded. The government announces it will seek financial assistance from the EU.

FACTS AT YOUR FINGERTIPS

GEOGRAPHY

Official name: Kingdom of Spain (Reino de España in Spanish)

Area: 195,124 square miles (505,370 sq km)

Climate: clear, hot summers in interior, more moderate and cloudy along coast; cloudy, cold winters in interior, partly cloudy and cool along coast

Highest elevation: Pico del Teide (Tenerife) on the Canary Islands, 12,198 feet (3,718 m) above sea level

Lowest elevation: Atlantic Ocean, 0 feet (0 m) below sea level

Significant geographic features: Rock of Gibraltar, Pyrenees Mountains

PEOPLE

Population (July 2012 est.):
47,042,984

Most populous city: Madrid

Ethnic groups: a mixture of
Mediterranean and Nordic types

Percentage of residents living in
urban areas: 77 percent

Life expectancy: 81.27 years at birth
(world rank 15)

Languages: Castilian Spanish, 74
percent; Catalan, 17 percent;
Galician, 7 percent; Basque, 2
percent.

Religion: Roman Catholic, 94
percent; other, 6 percent

GOVERNMENT AND ECONOMY

Government: parliamentary
monarchy

Capital: Madrid

Date of adoption of current
constitution: December 27, 1978

Head of state: king

Head of government: prime
minister

Legislature: National Assembly,
consisting of Senate and Congress
of Deputies

Currency: euro

Industries and natural resources:
textiles, food, metals, chemicals,
shipbuilding, automobiles, tourism,
pharmaceuticals

NATIONAL SYMBOLS

Holidays: October 12, Spanish National Day; December, 6; Constitution Day

Flag: three horizontal bands of red, yellow (double width), and red, with the national coat of arms on the hoist side of the yellow band

National anthem: "Himno Nacional Español" (National Anthem of Spain)

National animal: Spanish bull

KEY PEOPLE

King Juan Carlos I (1938–), hereditary king of Spain, was instrumental in creating a parliamentary monarchy

Generalissimo Francisco Franco (1892–1975), the dictator who ruled Spain harshly from 1939 to 1975.

REGIONS AND AUTONOMOUS CITIES OF SPAIN

Region; Capital

Andalusia; Seville

Asturias; Oviedo

Aragon; Zaragoza

Balearic Islands; Palma

Basque Country; Vitoria-Gasteiz

Canary Islands; Santa Cruz de Tenerife/Las Palmas

Cantabria; Santander

Castile-La Mancha; Toledo

Castile and León; Valladolid

Catalonia; Barcelona

Extremadura; Mérida

Galicia; Santiago de Compostela

La Rioja; Logroño

Madrid; Madrid

Murcia; Murcia

Navarre; Pamplona

Valencia; Valencia

Autonomous Cities

Ceuta

Melilla

GLOSSARY

ancestry

A person's family background or ethnic origin.

aristocratic

Belonging to a ruling class or the nobility.

autonomous

Acting independently, self-governing.

castanet

A percussion instrument typically used by dancers.

deficit

The amount by which something, especially an amount of money, is too small.

desertification

The process of once-fertile land becoming a desert.

dictator

A ruler with total control over a country, whose power has usually been achieved through force.

emissions

The production and discharge of something, especially a gas or a type of radiation.

endemic

>   Native to a certain area and found only in that area.

espresso

>   Strong black coffee made by forcing steam through ground coffee beans.

figurehead

>   A leader or head of state with no real power, who functions only as a symbol.

heresy

>   A belief or opinion that doesn't agree with orthodox religious beliefs.

proximity

>   Nearness in space, time, or relationship.

ADDITIONAL RESOURCES

SELECTED BIBLIOGRAPHY

Hooper, John. *The New Spaniards, 2nd Edition*. New York: Penguin, 2006. Print.

Inman, Nick et al. *Eyewitness Travel Guides: Spain*. New York: DK, 2011. Print.

Meany, Marian. *Culture Shock: Spain*. London: Kuperard, 2006. Print.

Phillips, William D. *A Concise History of Spain*. New York: Cambridge UP, 2010. Print.

FURTHER READINGS

Griffin, Julia Ortiz and William D. Griffin. *Spain and Portugal: A Reference Guide From The Renaissance To The Present*. New York: Facts On File, 2007. Print.

Stoff, Laurie. *A History of Nations: Spain*. Farmington Hills, MI: Greenhaven, 2004. Print.

WEB LINKS

To learn more about Spain, visit ABDO Publishing Company online at **www.abdopublishing.com**. Web sites about Spain are featured on our Book Links page. These links are routinely monitored and updated to provide the most current information available.

PLACES TO VISIT

If you are ever in Spain, consider checking out these important and interesting sites!

Alhambra Palace and Generalife Gardens, Granada

See a Moorish-style palace dating from the nineteenth century, featuring beautiful formal gardens and fountains.

Museo del Prado, Madrid

Spain's famous art museum features works by Goya and Velázquez.

Rock of Gibraltar

Visit this rocky island, explore the tunnels and galleries carved out of the rock, and watch ship traffic in the Strait of Gibraltar.

SOURCE NOTES

CHAPTER 1. A VISIT TO SPAIN

1. "What Is the Biggest Palace in Europe?" *Ask Yahoo*. Yahoo, 28 Apr. 2004. Web. 4 Oct. 2012.

2. "Gibraltar." *Encyclopædia Britannica*. Encyclopædia Britannica, 2012. Web. 4 Oct. 2012.

3. "The World Factbook: Gibraltar." *Central Intelligence Agency*. Central Intelligence Agency, 12 Sept. 2012. Web. 4 Oct. 2012.

CHAPTER 2. GEOGRAPHY: A DIVERSE PENINSULA

1. "The World Factbook: Spain." *Central Intelligence Agency*. Central Intelligence Agency, 12 Sept. 2012. Web. 4 Oct. 2012.

2. Ibid.

3. Ibid.

4. "Ebro River." *Encyclopædia Britannica*. Encyclopædia Britannica, 2012. Web. 8 Oct. 2012.

5. Ibid.

6. "The World Factbook: Spain." *Central Intelligence Agency*. Central Intelligence Agency, 12 Sept. 2012. Web. 8 Oct. 2012.

7. "Ibiza." *Holiday Weather*. Holiday Weather, 2012. Web. 8 Oct. 2012.

8. "Spain." *Weatherbase*. Canty and Associates, 2012. Web. 8 Oct. 2012.

CHAPTER 3. ANIMALS AND NATURE: SPECIES IN DANGER

1. Helen J. Temple and Annabelle Cuttelod. "The Status and Distribution of Mediterranean Mammals." *IUCN*. IUCN, 2009. Web. 8 Oct. 2012.

2. "Summary Statistics: Summaries by Country, Table 5, Threatened Species in Each Country." *IUCN Red List of Threatened Species*. International Union for Conservation of Nature and Natural Resources, 2011. Web. 8 Oct. 2012.

3. "Iberian Lynx." *WWF*. WWF, n.d. Web. 8 Oct. 2012.

4. "Spain 'To Fight Desertification' with 45m Trees." *ABC News*. ABC, 13 Sept. 2008. Web. 8 Oct. 2012.

5. "Spanish National Parks." *Spanish Institute of Tourism*. Spanish Institute of Tourism, 2012. Web. 8 Oct. 2012.

CHAPTER 4. HISTORY: FROM EMPIRES TO A REPUBLIC

1. Don Eiler. "Islam Comes to Europe." *Saudi Aramco World*. Saudi Aramco World, 2010. Web. 8 Oct. 2012.

2. Ibid.

3. "Spanish Judge Opens Case into Franco's Atrocities." *New York Times*. New York Times, 16 Oct. 2008. Web. 8 Oct. 2012.

4. "NATO Member Countries." *NATO*. NATO, 10 Mar. 2009. Web. 8 Oct. 2012.

CHAPTER 5. PEOPLE: UNITED DIVERSITY

1. "The World Factbook: Spain." *Central Intelligence Agency*. Central Intelligence Agency, 12 Sept. 2012. Web. 8 Oct. 2012.

2. Ibid.

3. Ibid.

4. Ibid.

5. Robert Manchin. "Religion in Europe: Trust Not Filling the Pews." *Gallup*. Gallup, 21 Sept. 2004. Web. 8 Oct. 2012.

6. "The World Factbook: Spain." *Central Intelligence Agency*. Central Intelligence Agency, 12 Sept. 2012. Web. 8 Oct. 2012.

7. Ibid.

8. Ibid.

9. Ibid.

10. Ibid.

CHAPTER 6. CULTURE: BEYOND BULLFIGHTS

1. Norman Lebrecht. "Domingo's Number—The One He Wants to Be Remembered By." *Slipped Disc*. Arts Journal, 3 July 2011. Web. 9 Oct. 2012.

SOURCE NOTES CONTINUED

CHAPTER 7. POLITICS: A MODERN MONARCHY

1. "General Elections 2011." *El País.* El País, 2011. Web. 9 Oct. 2012.

2. "What Is Eta?" *BBC News.* BBC, 20 Oct. 2011. Web. 9 Oct. 2012.

3. "Madrid Train Attacks." *BBC News Special Reports.* BBC, 14 Feb. 2007. Web. 9 Oct. 2012.

CHAPTER 8. ECONOMICS: MONEY TROUBLES

1. "Unemployment Rate – Seasonally Adjusted Data." *Google Public Data.* Eurostat, 1 Oct. 2012. Web. 9 Oct. 2012.

2. Ibid.

3. Jennifer Riggins. "Despite Economy, Spanish Tourism Prospers." *SmartPlanet.* CBS, 30 Jan. 2012. Web. 9 Oct. 2012.

4. "Spain Exports." *Trading Economics.* Trading Economics, 2012. Web. 9 Oct. 2012.

5. "The World Factbook: Spain." *Central Intelligence Agency.* Central Intelligence Agency, 12 Sept. 2012. Web. 9 Oct. 2012.

6. Ibid.

7. Ibid.

8. Raphael Minder. "Spanish Unemployment Rate Rises to 22.8 Percent." *New York Times.* New York Times, 27 Jan. 2012. Web. 9 Oct. 2012.

9. Ibid.

10. "The World Factbook: Spain." *Central Intelligence Agency.* Central Intelligence Agency, 12 Sept. 2012. Web. 9 Oct. 2012.

11. Patrick Allen. "Spain's Biggest Export, Young People." *CNBC.* CNBC, 8 Apr. 2011. Web. 9 Oct. 2012.

12. "Harmonised Unemployment Rate By Sex." *Eurostat.* Eurostat, 2012. Web. 9 Oct. 2012.

13. "Evolution (2004–2011) of the Poverty Hazard Rate by Age and Sex." *Instituto Nacional de Estadística.* Instituto Nacional de Estadística, 2012. Web. 9 Oct. 2012.

14. Ibid.

CHAPTER 9. SPAIN TODAY

1. "The World Factbook: Spain." *Central Intelligence Agency*. Central Intelligence Agency, 12 Sept. 2012. Web. 9 Oct. 2012.

2. "Teenage Issues." *Anglo Info Spain*. Anglo Info, 2012. Web. 9 Oct. 2012.

INDEX

Albayzín, 10
Alfonso XIII, King, 57, 61
Alhambra Palace, 8, 10, 79
Almodóvar, Pedro, 83
Altamira Cave, 42
Amenábar, Alejandro, 83
Andorra, 17
animals, 29–34, 39, 84, 88
architecture, 8, 79, 109–110
area, 15, 17–18
arts, 75–83
Atlantis, 37

Balearic Islands, 17–18, 24, 25, 65
Banderas, Antonio, 34
Barbary macaque, 30–32
Barcelona, 12, 20, 22, 68, 76, 79
Bardem, Javier, 83
Basque, 18, 20, 65, 91, 96, 101, 102, 118
birds, 29, 32, 33, 39
Biscay, Bay of, 17
bordering countries, 17
bullfighting, 29, 84, 86–88
bulls, 29, 84, 86–88
Buñuel, Luis, 83

Calderón, José, 91
Canary Islands, 18, 24, 26, 33, 39, 88
Cantabrian Mountains, 23, 41
Carlist Wars, 54

Carlos V, 54
Catalonia, 12, 18, 20, 65, 84, 88, 101, 118
Cela, Camilo José, 76, 79
Cervantes, Miguel de, 76
Charles II, King, 53
climate, 11, 26, 30, 37, 112
Columbus, Christopher, 51–53
constitution, 20, 54, 61, 65–66, 84, 93–96, 99, 100–101
Cuban War of Independence, 57
currency, 15, 109–110

Dalí, Salvador, 75–76, 83
dance, 7, 79–80
Domingo, Plácido, 80
Don Quixote, 76
drug trafficking, 122, 124

Ebro River, 23, 25
economic growth, 58, 105–106
education, 72, 118–121
endangered species, 30, 32, 33, 34, 39
environmental threats, 38–39, 124–126
esparto grass, 37
ethnic groups, 63
European Union, 61, 71, 105–106, 109, 112–115, 124

Euskadi Ta Askatasuna, 102
exports, 106

families, 71–72, 122, 126
Ferdinand, King, 51, 66
fish, 18, 32–33, 84, 106, 112
flag, 94
food, 84–86, 106, 109
France, 12, 17, 45, 53–54, 102, 105, 109
Franco, Francisco, 58–61, 71, 76, 80, 83, 101

Galicia, 18, 65
Gibraltar, 10, 12, 17, 30–32, 46, 49, 54
gold, 42, 45
government structure, 15, 20, 93, 96–101
Goya, Francisco de, 7, 75
Granada, 8–10, 23, 49, 51, 79
Great Britain, 45, 53–54
Greeks, 42
gross domestic product, 15, 121

holidays, 83–84
Holy Roman Empire, 45–46, 53, 88

Iberian lynx, 30, 33–34
Iberian Mountains, 23
Iberian Peninsula, 7, 17, 18, 23, 29, 42–46, 86
Iglesias, Enrique, 83

Iglesias, Julio, 83
imports, 109, 110
independence, 94–96
industries, 49, 80, 83,
    105–106, 110
International Union for
    Conservation of Nature,
    29, 32
Isabella, Queen, 49–51, 66

Juan Carlos I, 61, 94, 102

Kyoto Protocol, 126

language, 15, 63–66
Las Médulas, 45
leaders, current, 102
life expectancy, 68
literacy rate, 118
literature, 49, 76–79
Lorca, Federico García, 76

Madrid, 7–8, 10, 15, 18,
    20–22, 26, 68, 79, 102
Mediterranean monk seal, 33
Mediterranean Sea, 11–12,
    17–18, 23, 26, 38
Meseta, 23, 26, 34
Miró, Joan, 75
Moors, 8–10, 30, 46–51, 63,
    66, 76
Morocco, 10, 18, 32
mountains, 12, 17, 23–24,
    30–32, 34–37, 39, 41

music, 7, 79–83
Muslims, 8–10, 46–49, 51, 68,
    102

National Assembly, 97–99
national capital, 7, 15, 20, 26
national parks, 37, 38–39
natural resources, 45

official name, 15

Peninsular War, 54
Philip II, King, 53
Philip V, King, 53
Phoenicians, 42
Pica d'Estats, 12
Picasso, Pablo, 75
plants, 32, 34–37
political parties, 57–58, 94,
    97, 101–102
population, 15, 68
Portugal, 17, 53–54
poverty, 115
Primo de Riviera, Miguel, 57
Punic Wars, 45
Pyrenees, 12, 17, 23, 34

Rajoy, Mariano, 102
regions, 11–12, 18–20, 26, 30,
    34, 38, 63, 65, 84–85, 88,
    91, 96–99, 101, 118, 126
religion, 15, 66–68, 83–84,
    94–96
rivers, 23, 25, 32, 45
Romans, 18, 30, 45–46, 53,
    63, 86

Royal Palace, 7, 79
Rubio, Ricky, 91

Segovia, Andrés, 80
Seville, 23, 79
Sierra Nevada Mountains, 23
siesta, 68, 117
Spanish Civil War, 57–58,
    66, 76
Spanish imperial eagle, 29, 33
Spanish Inquisition, 51
Spanish-American War, 57
sports, 86–91

Tàpies, Antoni, 75–76
teenage life, 117–118, 122–124
terrorism, 102
tourism, 8, 84, 96, 106, 110

unemployment, 105–106,
    110, 112, 115, 122, 124
UNESCO World Heritage
    Sites, 38

Valencia, 11–12, 18, 23, 65, 68
Visigoths, 46, 63
volcanoes, 24, 39

War of Spanish Succession,
    53
women, 65, 71–72
World War I, 57
World War II, 58

Zafón, Carlos Ruiz, 79

PHOTO CREDITS

Luciano Mortula/Shutterstock Images, cover; Paul White/AP Images, 2, 62; Rafa Irusta/ Shutterstock Images, 5 (top), 35; Alex Tihonovs/Shutterstock Images, 5 (center), 11; Shutterstock Images, 5 (bottom), 6, 8, 16, 21, 22, 24, 28, 39, 40, 67, 74, 77, 87, 108, 130; Matt Kania/Map Hero, Inc., 13, 19, 27, 70, 107; Ingvar Bjork/Shutterstock Images, 31; Matyas Arvai/ Shutterstock Images, 36; Aranberri/AP Images, 43; Alberto Loyo/Shutterstock Images, 44; North Wind Picture Archives, 47, 48, 52, 128 ; Holger W./Shutterstock Images, 50; José Casado del Alisal, 55; Bettmann/Corbis/AP Images, 56, 59, 129 (top); Jockel Finck/AP Images, 60; AISPIX by Image Source/Shutterstock Images, 69; Kike Calvo/AP Images, 73; Manu Fernandez/AP Images, 78, 120; La Tercera/AP Images, 81; Miramax/Everett Collection, 82; Moises Fernandez Acosta/ Shutterstock Images, 85; Mark Ralston/AP Images, 89; Bob Edme/AP Images, 90; Rafael Ramirez Lee/Shutterstock Images, 92; rSnapshotPhotos/Shutterstock Images, 95, 132; Peter Macdiarmid/ AP Images, 98, 131; Denis Doyle/AP Images, 100; Angel Diaz/AP Images, 103; Alberto Di Lolli/ AP Images, 104, 129 (bottom); Lilie Graphie/Shutterstock Images, 111; Vitaly Titov & Maria Sidelnikova/Shutterstock Images, 113; Andres Kudacki/AP Images, 114; iStockphoto, 116; Daniel Ochoa de Olza/AP Images, 119; Ana del Castillo/Shutterstock Images, 123; KarSol/Shutterstock Images, 125; Emilio Morenatti/AP Images, 127